IN THE ABSENCE OF PARADISE

THE ART OF DAVID BIERK

THE TELLEM PRESS, OTTAWA
THE ART GALLERY OF PETERBOROUGH

ACKNOWLEDGEMENTS

This book is the product of the dedication and generous efforts of many individuals to whom I am very grateful.

In particular I would like to thank: Illi-Maria Tamplin, Director of the Art Gallery of Peterborough, whose understanding of my work and ideas has enhanced this book immeasurably; Dennis Tourbin, for his continuous editorial assistance and for his steadfast friendship and enthusiasm throughout the projects of my life and art; Daniel Sharp, friend and fellow-artist, for his curatorial perspectives and insights; Gary Michael Dault, for his persistence with the fictitious film script, which may someday find its way onto celluloid; Doug Chomyn, for his design of this book in the face of my ever changing ideas; Peter Ramsay, for his help and advice in the printing process; Jan Turner and Diane Farris, for opening the doors; Lynne Wynick and David Tuck, for their deep and ongoing commitment to me and my work; Pablo, my assistant, whose untiring efforts make what I do possible; Doris Bierk, my mother, for giving me the determination to pursue my life's dreams; my parents-in-law, Cotton and Jeff Aimers, for their unfailing support and inspiration; and my children, Bass, Heather, Zac, Jeff, Alex, Nicky and Charlie, for enthusiastically sharing this career and life.

Finally, this book is dedicated with love to my wife and partner, Liz, who has not only worked tirelessly on this project but without whom none of it would have any meaning. — DAVID BIERK

The essay entitled 'David Bierk: Observer, Painter, Curator, Realist, Romantic, Dreamer, or How does Photography, that Secondary Reality, Feed the Primary Reality of Painting?' by Illi-Maria Tamplin first appeared in the catalogue which accompanied the exhibition 'David Bierk: In the Absence of Paradise', at the Art Gallery of Peterborough in 1991.

The poem entitled '[David Bierk:] A Portrait' by Dennis Tourbin was written for the catalogue which accompanied the exhibition 'David Bierk: Ten Years', at the Art Gallery of Peterborough in 1981.

COVER PAINTING: *To Manet and Vermeer*, 1989, oil on canvas, plaster on plywood. 44½" x 70". Collection: Carole and Jerry Isenberg, Beverly Hills, Calif.

Published by The Tellem Press in cooperation with The Art Gallery of Peterborough, Peterborough, Ontario, Canada.

The financial contribution of the Government of Canada made possible from the Department of Communications through the PADAC Art Foundation is acknowledged.

The Tellem Press
P.O. Box 4816, Station 'E'
Ottawa, Ontario
Canada K1S 5H9

Colour separations and electronic pre-press by Studio Colour Group Inc., Ottawa.
Printed in Canada by Dollco Printing, Ottawa.

CANADIAN CATALOGUING IN PUBLICATION DATA
Main entry under title:

In the absence of paradise: the art of David Bierk.

ISBN 1-895286-01-8

1. Bierk, David, 1944- – Criticism and interpretation. I. Tamplin, Illi-Maria   II. Art Gallery of Peterborough.

ND249.B534 1993   709'.2   C93 – 090621 – 7

Home/Wife, to Vermeer
oil on photomontage on canvas
73" x 52"
1989
Collection: Evander Schley, Malibu, Calif.

CONTENTS

The phrase IN THE ABSENCE OF PARADISE was coined by curator Daniel Sharp as the title for an exhibition of my work at Gallery 101 in Ottawa in 1988. It quickly became part of the thought and vocabulary of my work and was incorporated into the titles of a series of paintings I produced in 1990. The appeal of this phrase lies in its literal and conceptual application to my work, a nostalgia for a vision of life untroubled and sublime, and at the same time a condemnation of what the twentieth-century vision of progress has imposed on the world. 'In the absence of paradise' refers equally to my sense in art of the exhaustion of pure creative invention and the corollary loss, in painting, of a certain place of authority in today's culture. Paradoxically, the longing for a lost art and life that embody virtue and the qualities of humanism and heroism is not entirely melancholic. It is very much intended as a positive step towards in some way improving the situation. For this publication, the documentation of an artist working at the end of the century, it seemed fitting to return to the phrase 'in the absence of paradise' as a means of linking the various elements of my work and life which follow. — D.B.

Cape Breton Morning Fog
oil on canvas
60½" x 87"
1987
Collection: Home Savings of America,
Irwindale, Calif.

4

DAVID BIERK

OBSERVER, PAINTER, CURATOR, REALIST,

ROMANTIC, DREAMER,

or

HOW DOES PHOTOGRAPHY, THAT SECONDARY REALITY,

FEED THE PRIMARY REALITY OF PAINTING?

by Illi-Maria Tamplin

In Search of the American Dream

(installation view)

oil on canvas

288" x 192"

1971

WHEN DAVID BIERK arrived in this community twenty years ago, he brought with him an entrepreneurial attitude that said anything is possible if you set your sights high and work very hard. Bierk became an adult in California in the mid-1960s, then lived in the Bahamas for a short time, moving to Peterborough, Ontario, Canada in 1971. He successfully mixed an all-American work ethic, a cocky optimism and free-form pluralism learned in the 1960s with the ability to adapt to the new homeland. This vital combination gives him the edge to survive as an artist. But Bierk does not merely survive in a small Canadian city: he succeeds in presenting his work on the international art scene.

Bierk's career spans more than twenty-five years and carries the plurality of images and ideas associated with post-modern times which are our times, even now. The kingpin in the compilation of information which results in the reality of Bierk's painting and image making is the photograph – that secondary reality. Bierk, like many artists today, shows no inhibition in utilizing in his paintings the photographic images generated by himself, by popular culture, by the media or by reproduction of artworks from distant cultures and by other artists. Neither does Bierk hesitate to create new media permutations, such as the recent painted photograph, a hybrid of paint and the pristine surface of his landscape Cibachromes.

A surprised Peterborough audience was confronted by a very large painting by David Bierk in the exhibition *Monument to Miniature*, 1975, organized by him for the Market Hall space prior to its becoming Artspace in Peterborough Square. The twenty-four foot high painting called *In Search of the American Dream*, 1971, features a giant image of the American child film star Shirley Temple. In front of her stand rows and rows of monochrome people. It is perhaps easier to trace the reasons for our audience's puzzlement in retrospect. With respect to the size of the image, local people would have been familiar with such images on outdoor advertising posters – the Shirley Temple image did indeed come from a poster. But to see her face enlarged to huge proportions with very white smiling teeth, the famous dimples and sparkling eyes looking down from a painting in an art exhibition was a new experience.

The image source for the group of people in the foreground of the painting is a 1940s panoramic photo of Canadian teachers at a convention. In the painting, these figures are as large as the viewer who therefore cannot escape from becoming, by proximity and association, a part of this grey and impersonal gathering. Our Peterborough audience might also have found it rather disconcerting that the suggested avenue of escape from the ordinariness of it all was to fall under the spell of a child superstar and 'the American Dream'.

In larger urban centres, audiences might have been visually prepared for Bierk's *In Search of the American Dream* by experiencing such photographic exhibitions as *The Family of Man*, organized in 1955 by The Museum of Modern Art in New York and circulated simultaneously by means of photographic multiples to several cities, with the tour extending well into the 1960s. This exhibition contained photographic blow-ups of the people of the world. The size of the photographs sometimes reached mural dimensions. The multiplicity of photographic images as legitimate museum objects worth displaying had led the way for the introduction of the multiple art object created by Pop artists like Andy Warhol as part of the new popular culture. Bierk's recreation of the Shirley Temple poster introduced the Pop Art image to Peterborough in an undeniably monumental way.

The controversy of whether photographs in themselves are indeed original works of art in the 'high' art sense has raged throughout this century in museums and in critical writings on art. Even in the nineteenth century, not long after the photographic process was invented, Charles Baudelaire examined the nature and function of photographs and their relationship to art. He advocated that photography's most appropriate use should be as a subservient tool, and it has become just that for many artists today.

In *The Salon of 1859*, Baudelaire writes about 'The Modern Public and Photography':

> If photography is allowed to supplement art in some of its functions, it will soon have supplanted or corrupted it altogether, thanks to the stupidity of the multitude which is its natural ally. It is time, then, for it to return to its true duty, which is to be the servant of the sciences and arts – but the very humble servant, like printing or shorthand, which have neither created nor supplemented literature.

Baudelaire goes on to suggest various uses for photography. The following among them is of particular interest in relation to the idea of 'A Museum Without Walls' as proposed in the book of that name by André Malraux[1] and that concept's application in the paintings of David Bierk.

Let it (photography) rescue from oblivion those tumbling ruins, those books, prints and manuscripts which time is devouring, precious things whose form is dissolving and which demand a place in the archives of our memory – it will be thanked and applauded.[2]

In our century, the systematic proliferation of photographic reproduction of those 'precious things' has certainly rescued many of them from oblivion. Artworks which reside in museums or those which are inaccessible in old churches or on distant mountaintops have through photography become popular images and in our society have entered the realm of common knowledge. Through the photographic image, these objects are also now shared across cultural borders and are consumed on a daily basis, instead of once in a lifetime by pilgrimage to their actual location. Students tape the images on their locker doors, affluent people frame them in gold, publishers fill coffee table books with them and artists pin them on their studio walls. We have indeed become so accustomed to viewing art by means of photographically reproduced images that we totally accept reality's cousin once or even twice removed from the source. In André Malraux's vision, all artworks which can be photographically reproduced become part of 'the same family' and in that photographic state can be submitted to curatorial manipulation by everyone.

But artists like David Bierk who engage in a kind of curatorial selection process, claim certain 'public domain' images from our vast morass of information and make them into the reality of their own work. Already in 1975, Bierk used appropriated elements in the painting *Hockey Night in Canada,* at a time when that now frequently used word 'appropriation' had rarely been whispered within art circles. In that painting, he links our obsession with viewing television, particularly the Saturday night ritual in Canada of watching hockey games, to the religious experience of standing before the image of God as represented in

the Ghent altarpiece which was completed in Flanders by the van Eyck brothers in the year 1432.

The idea of using reproductions of old master paintings from the large encyclopedia of available images and incorporating them in collages, paintings or prints was prevalent in the work of the 1960s, especially in Britain and the United States. Bierk would have been aware of the work of well-publicized heroes of the day, such as the American artist Robert Rauschenberg who in his work made comments about art, culture and society through a complex juxtaposition of objects and images. For instance, Rubens' *Venus at her Toilet*, a 'pin-up' on Rauschenberg's studio wall, floats easily in its entirety from that wall onto his paintings and photomontages. As Douglas Crimp points out in his essay 'On the Museum's Ruins':

Rauschenberg had moved definitely from techniques of *production* (combines, assemblages) to techniques of *reproduction* (silk-screens, transfer drawings). And it is this move that requires us to think of Rauschenberg's art as post-modernist. Through reproductive technology post-modernist art dispenses with the aura. The fiction of creating subject gives way to the frank confiscation, quotation, excerptation, accumulation and repetition of already existing images. Notions of originality, authenticity and presence, essential to the ordered discourse of the museum, are undermined.[3]

As far as *Hockey Night in Canada* is concerned, the fact of the matter is of course that in 1975 David Bierk was not in Ghent, but in his studio in Peterborough referring to a photographic reproduction of the Ghent altarpiece in a book. Looking at his painting *Hockey Night In Canada*, we immediately recognize Hubert and Jan van Eyck's famous, realistic rendering of Adam and Eve. But since Bierk quoted only those two figures directly out of a very large array of figures in the original work, it was necessary to look at the reproduction of the original again just to refresh our memory. Having had the experience of standing before the Ghent altarpiece, my personal memory of its size and three-dimensionality interfered in this exercise of visual retrieval and comparison and needed to be counteracted. By placing a black and white photograph of Bierk's painting next to a black and white image of the Ghent altarpiece reproduced with its doors open, flat on the page of a

book, one seems to achieve the proper neutrality and sense of 'the same family' of image required for this equation.

Then, having set aside Bierk's outrageous tongue-in-cheek comment on our society and revelled in the delicious parody, we can begin to examine the composition. The figures of Eve and Adam in *Hockey Night in Canada* have been mirror reversed, possibly because of the mechanics of transposing the images, but more likely with intent, since this also makes them turn their backs on the central image of adoration. The centre panel of the small bejewelled altar floating in the sky contains hockey players in a joyful victory embrace. The successful player and hero of the moment reaches out to us with a gloved hand, imitating the exact pose of the Almighty's right hand raised in a gesture of benediction in the Ghent altar. Below on the horizon are ordinary farm buildings and in

Hockey Night in Canada
oil on canvas,
mixed media collage
67½" x 84¾"
1975

9

the field peacefully grazing is a herd of ordinary cows, or perhaps even sacred cows. At the very bottom of the field is a chorus line of scantily clad young women hidden among the grasses. They are cut-outs transposed from underwear advertisements which are now stand-ins for the chorus of angels. A band of brightly lit sky separates the earthbound elements from those inhabiting the heavens and replicates the same compositional device of the original altarpiece.

The landscape portion of the composition is based on a photograph taken by Bierk of our rural Ontario surroundings. It refers and anchors the painting to a particular reality we share. The three borrowed images – the Ontario landscape, the figures from the Ghent altarpiece and the television picture from the programme *Hockey Night in Canada* – manage, by means of the photographic transfer, to shake off the primary meaning of their existence and assume a plausible new reality in the painting.

In relation to another work, a snapshot taken in the Bahamas pictures a sumptuous feast laid on a table before David Bierk and his extended family, seated against a backdrop of lush vegetation. In 1975, now living in Canada, David Bierk paints *A Shared Dream: Homage to Henri Rousseau, The Canadian Indian, Charlie Brown, Leonardo da Vinci, Larry Poons, Larry Gray, the California Grape and Fine Art in general*. Initially, Bierk's painting may have been stimulated by the impact of the Bahamian landscape with its abundant palm trees and the congenial atmosphere of the family gathering. But in the composition of the painting, Bierk substitutes for the natural background his personal rendition of Henri Rousseau's 1910 painting *The Dream*. The central figure in the snapshot, his brother-in-law, no longer a member of the family in 1975, has been replaced by an Indian man called Old Crow. The whole group is placed on a carpeted platform with a decorative border of actual feathers and tusks attached to the bottom of the canvas. The family group together with the Rousseau painting seem to be floating among clouds.

This time, the composition is based on two photographs, one a record of a family meal and the other a reproduction of Rousseau's painting. The family members and friends have been snapped in a stereotypical way. The photograph on its own serves the customary function of recording the event. In her essay *Photography and the Simulacral*, Rosalind Krauss tells us that according to sociologist Pierre Bourdieu in his study *Un art moyen*, Paris, 1965:

> Photography as an *art moyen*, a practice carried out by the average man, must be defined in terms of its social functions. These functions he sees as wholly connected to the structure of the family in the modern world, with the family photograph an index or proof of family unity … The photographic record is part of the point of these family gatherings; it is an agent in the collective fantasy of family cohesion, and in that sense the camera is a projective tool, part of the theatre that the family constructs to convince itself that it is together and whole. 'Photography itself,' Bourdieu writes, 'is most frequently nothing but the *re*production of the image that a group produces of its own integration.'[4]

If David Bierk had taken this photograph and pasted it into an album, the reason for this image would have fitted exactly with the one described above. But Bierk altered the simple purpose of the family snapshot by translating it into the medium of paint, by changing its size, by placing the 'theatre that the family constructs' on a different stage and presenting a totally new, all-encompassing kind of 'integration' for the family. The presence of the native man, the Eve-like figure and black flute player in Rousseau's painting expands the 'family' idea to include a larger world family, perhaps even past cultures who have gone before us. The homage to Leonardo da Vinci in the title of the work adds to the compositional clues that place us in the presence of some kind of last supper, perhaps commemorating a lost paradise. Such ecologically connected comments will resurface frequently in Bierk's later work.

In 1974, David Bierk worked on a series called *Heroes* and on another titled *Friends*. With these unusual works he experimented with a complex succession of image transfers which pass through several states of being second and third cousins to the original source image. In a work such as *"Intricate beadwork emblazons the regalia of 90-year-old Chief Sitting Eagle of the Assiniboine, or Stoney tribe, during an annual festival at Banff"*, the source image comes from an ordinary reproduction in a book. But in order to give this figure 'hero' status, Bierk photographs it and makes a slide which is then projected on a

television screen. The television image with its moiré pattern resulting from the horizontal scanning lines on the screen is then duplicated on the back of a piece of plexiglas with serigraphy and paint. Giving this simulated 'television' look to the image has put Sitting Eagle, a hero from far away and perhaps from long ago, through a time warp and presented him to us with an immediacy only television images can produce.

Bierk's facility in handling various painting techniques has always been a great asset in adapting the appropriate medium to the subject matter. In the 1975 work *Laundromat, Canadian Interior*, he paints the image in the Photo-Realist style. Photo-Realism became prevalent in the mid-1960s and flourished in the 1970s. It was another way painters tried to win back some of the domain garnered by photography. This time it was achieved through surpassing the realism possible in photography by heightening the intensity of the painted surface to achieve a super-real image. Artists researched early painting techniques of egg tempera or oil glazes resulting in very thin paint applications which emulated the photograph's own smooth surface and at the same time allowed for superior illusions of depth and perspective. Photo-Realists like the American painter Richard Estes preferred to depict the slick surfaces of contemporary urban subjects. For David Bierk the interior of a laundromat, with its smooth tile floor and shiny metal surfaces, was an appropriate challenge in this medium.

But in addition to the Photo-Realist aspects, Bierk again introduces an appropriated image of an old master work, *Madonna of Canon van der Paele* by Jan van Eyck. By tilting the van Eyck painting backwards into the composition, Bierk also alludes to the painting *The Ambassadors* by Hans Holbein the Younger (1497-1543) where a trick mirror is tilted to show a greatly foreshortened skull. The reason for this illusionistic tour de force in the Holbein painting is left to conjecture. However, the detailed rendering of objects in the Holbein painting

Laundromat, Canadian Interior

oil on canvas

5' x 7'

1975

Collection: Art Gallery of Peterborough, Peterborough, Ont.

One Year Later … Homage to John Lennon, the Number 9, the Solar System, Paul Gauguin, Emile Zola, Vincent van Gogh, Claude Monet, Gustave Courbet, Ingres, Sir Lawrence Alma Tadema, and John Heartfield

acrylic and watercolour on canvas

9' x 9'

1981

Collection: Art Gallery of Peterborough, Peterborough, Ont.

certainly advertised his skill as do those in Bierk's work. In *Laundromat, Canadian Interior*, the triangular composition of a contemporary nuclear family standing in the laundromat balances the van Eyck painting of the holy family hovering just above the tiled floor. The man and woman gaze vaguely in the direction of the boy who looks directly at the viewer; all three seem to be oblivious of the holy image at their feet. The appropriated image of the Jan van Eyck painting remains fully integrated into the composition and continues to contribute symbolically to the meaning of Bierk's work.

In the latter part of the 1970s, David Bierk frequently photographed the landscape, especially the ancient rock formations of the Pre-Cambrian Shield which begins just north and east of Peterborough. The series of paintings of rock faces based directly on these photographs continues the use of the Photo-Realist style. In 1980 Bierk shifted the idea of rock folds to painted folds on canvas. Although these 'fold' paintings were made by wrapping canvas over a solid object and spray painting the folds from different directions, the restretched, flat canvases still carry the illusions of depth of the Photo-Realist paintings. The wrapping idea also refers to the work of the artist Christo, who wrapped a number of important structures and landscapes and then exhibited the results of these ephemeral works through the records of films and photographs. In 1980 Bierk invited Christo to present his work in Peterborough.

Bierk again summons images from photo-based sources in a major work from 1981, *One Year Later*. In the construction of the nine paintings which make up this work, canvas is pulled over a circular shape to form the background. In the central circle, by means of a thin glazing technique, Bierk paints the smiling face of John Lennon, a year after his death and in the company of Emile Zola, Paul Gauguin, Vincent van Gogh, Claude Monet, Gustave Courbet, Ingres, Sir Lawrence Alma-Tadema and John Heartfield. It is an homage to Lennon and eight other luminaries admired by Bierk. The nine individual canvases hang in a grid formation, a compositional device used in other works by the artist. The grid also relates to the ancient method of transferring images from a drawing or large cartoon

To Alexander
oil on paper
30" x 40"
1987
Private collection

by imposing a grid over the image and then copying it, square by square. Even now, Bierk continues to use this method of image transfer and prefers it to the contemporary way of projecting slides onto canvas. Lately he has made the grid squares larger to encourage a looser handling of paint, which then allows for a more painterly and personally expressive brush stroke.

The sheer pleasure of using paint in a rich, multilayered way began to show in the landscape paintings of *The Save the Planet Imaginary Landscape Series* of 1984. During the early 1980s Bierk travelled by car to the west coast of Canada and the United States, to Newfoundland, to the Maritimes and the Eastern Townships of Quebec. From each trip he brought back photographs which captured glorious evening skies and spectacular cloud formations. Bierk also travelled along the Hudson River Valley and sought out the work of nineteenth-century American painters such as George Inness and Frederic Church. The Hudson River painters often chose high vantage points from which they could take in wide panoramic views and emphasize atmospheric cloud formations. The painter Pierre Charles

L'Enfant even taped three watercolours together in order to make up the widest possible vista of the spectacular scenery at West Point. Bierk made a point of visiting Frederic Church's studio, which has been preserved at Olana on the Hudson River, and photographed views of the river and the Catskill Mountains from there. He felt a close affinity with Church and admired his grandiose schemes of manipulating the landscape of Olana by creating actual lakes and ponds to balance the view of the Hudson River which Church would then paint. Bierk could manipulate landscapes more easily by fitting single photographs into panoramic collages without engaging in large earth moving projects. He altered and improved on the view to his heart's content. By choosing to depict very scenic, beautiful and romantic landscapes, Bierk aligns himself with the poetic painters of the mid-nineteenth century who regarded nature with reverence and as a direct manifestation of God.

In the 1985 painting *To Alexander*, Bierk introduces the head of a classical statue, painted in grey monochrome from a black and white reproduction, as an insert into the upper centre

of a very dark sky. There is little tonal difference between them and they meld together as one image, complement each other, brooding. This composition works very much as does that in the painting *Laundromat, Canadian Interior,* where the appropriated image is integrated with the overall composition through its compatibility of texture and colouring. Up to this point Bierk's borrowing methods are akin to those of painters who have gone before him. In the fascinating article 'Manet's Sources, Aspects of his Art, 1859-1865', *Artforum*, March, 1969[5], Michael Fried examines the way in which Manet extracted certain figures and compositions from artists of the past whose work he admired and wanted to connect with his own. Fried also points out that Manet's sources were not always taken directly from paintings, but were often derived from secondary images such as engravings and etchings of paintings by Raphael, Rubens or Watteau.

The same heroic head from *To Alexander,* 1985 is painted in a much larger, more prominent format in the 1987 painting

Alexander Contemplating Why U.F.O.s Don't Land Here Anymore: to Caspar David Friedrich, Albert Bierstadt, John William Casilear, Frederic Edwin Church and T.E. Pfliger. The head takes up a full two-thirds of the canvas and is quite distinct from the narrow third on the right of the canvas which shows four romantic landscapes stacked one above the other like frames from a filmstrip. The architectural remains in one of the landscapes refer to the imaginary archaeological models created by the artist Terry Pfliger. The petrified face of the statue with its stone cold eyes can no longer see or feel the heat of those landscapes. We may infer that an atomic blast has set the land ablaze and turned it into Sodom and Gomorrah and the human witness into stone. The ecological message is augmented by the depiction of Alexander, a classical hero who destroyed civilizations and land in the path of his conquests. Is our planet now in such a state that no one wants to land here anymore? Did our clouded view of Alexander as a hero and the romantic nineteenth-century atti-

tude to landscape in fact inhibit us from adopting an ecologically sound attitude toward our planet?

Since 1987 Bierk has favoured the splitting of his compositions into a diptych format, using one side for a landscape based on reproductions of the work of painters such as Constable, Keith, and Church and the other for a figurative work or detail by such old masters as Vermeer, Michelangelo, Leonardo da Vinci and Caravaggio. By abutting diverse self-contained images, he leaves us with no centre to the composition, a post-modern device which attempts to negate formalist aesthetics. Each side of the painting, almost equal in size, could stand on its own, but Bierk pairs them until their mood and colour are in sympathy with their companion in much the same way as illustrations on opposite pages in a book are separate but complement each other. The pairing process occurs after the proper amount of image research has taken place and the quotations from the works of previous masters have been selected. This split-screen compositional device counters the classical central focus composition which traditionally heightened conditions for drama and narrative. Bierk is still able to achieve much theatricality in paintings like *Autumn Light, to Inness and Vermeer*, 1988 and *Autumn Sunset, to Keith and Caravaggio*, 1989.

Since the mid-1980s Bierk has also painted several key compositions constructed on a variation of the triptych. *The Flash Art Triptych* of 1987 comes closest to its religious prototype. The central panel is taller than the side panels and shows the bold letters 'Flash Art' above a scene of the Last Supper painted by Andy Warhol. This image is flanked by the 'doors' painted with covers of *House and Garden* magazine which also use paintings for their illustrations, that on the left by David Hockney, that on the right by Claude Monet. Bierk then frames the three sections as one unit.

The trompe-l'oeil technique which Bierk uses in this work reminds us of his earlier Photo-Realist paintings and at the same time refers us back to seventeenth-century Dutch and nineteenth-century American artists who used this technique, which is meant to make the objects in the paintings so real that they will literally 'fool the eye'. But since that result can now be

Flash Art Triptych

oil on canvas and metal leaf

41" x 79"

1987

achieved more easily through colour photography, Bierk's intent cannot be read so simply. For one thing, the magazine covers have been enlarged, which gives them greater presence on the wall. An image scaled to be held in our hands has been removed from that intimate context and made monumental. Bierk's process of image displacement and translation in these 'covers' is similar to the television-related *Friends* and *Heroes* series. He takes a photo-based image of ordinary magazine proportions and gives it a new significance through altered scale, special placement and painting technique.

The magazine cover, a commodity which is in itself an object, is transformed through paint into a different object. Even though it still carries the same image, the physicality of the new object imposes another reality and therefore presents a new message. Magazines have had the power to change original art works of the 'high' art type into 'Pop' art items for wide public consumption. It is then left to Bierk to reconstitute the printed image and change it back to a painted art object, but not without the blemishes of magazine titles and bar codes. By leaving this detritus, he makes it impossible for us to wipe the slate clean. We are not forgiven for violating the once original, pristine and glorious painted masterpiece.

With the triptychs *Art in America*, 1987, *Art, Object, Commodity*, 1988, and *A Family Portrait, to the Bwami Tribe, Degas and Freud*, 1989, Bierk takes a curatorial step into the museum, assumes the role of presenter of objects and makes cross-cultural notations. In *A Family Portrait...*, the central panel, Degas' *The Bellelli Family*, 1860, is set between an African mask and a portrait of Freud. Degas had already created a painting with complex psychological tensions. Bierk takes this given and supplements it by choosing a mask surrounded by a dark background which echoes the face of the mother dressed in black as well as the daughters' faces. The grey photograph of Freud casts its analytical eye on us and balances the head of the father in Degas' painting, who is seated facing away from the viewer but watching his family with a sideward glance. Bierk has painted the head of the daughter in the centre in a blur, as happens in photographs when the sitter moves while the picture is taken. Since this girl also occupies the centre of the entire composition, her vacillating head pulls us into the circle of the group and manipulates the strings that make all the psychological connections possible.

The separate parts in the triptychs *Art in America* and *Art, Object, Commodity* look like a museum presentation of artifacts with their careful framing and means of attaching to the wall. Their appearance is linked to the work of American artist Louise Lawler, who since the late 1970s 'has made photographs and installations that focus critical attention on the institutionally

sanctioned mystique of museums and the objects they possess'. These two works by Bierk are like mini-museums sharing some of the attitudes toward presentation explored by Lawler. Trevor Fairbrother writes about her views on museum activities for the exhibition brochure *Connections: Louise Lawler*:

Lawler's concern for posing questions rather than giving answers results in a dialogue that is complicated and open-ended: she seeks to expose, debunk, and explicate the various meanings that art objects accumulate from the moment of creation and distribution to their permanent existence as things bought and sold, stored and displayed, written about and reproduced. Destroying what for some is a cherished illusion, she shows us that a museum is neither a haven of stability nor a neutral forum; rather, it is in a state of constant flux, and its collections and exhibitions reflect the shifting preferences, prejudices, and procedures of the institution, its officers and its staff.[6]

A Family Portrait,

to the Bwami tribe, Degas and Freud

oil on canvas

54" x 138"

1989

Collection: Central Guaranty Trust, Toronto, Ont.

Floral still-lifes like the one in the 1987 *Art in America* painting appear frequently in many of Bierk's paintings from the *In the Absence of Paradise* and *In the Absence of Virtue* series. Sometimes they are the full size of one of the diptych or triptych panels, while in other works they are small paintings set behind glass inside a plywood panel coated with gesso to look like a rough plaster wall and then painted a solid colour. This presentation makes them as precious and protected as some old master oil paintings which museums have for security reasons covered with glass. Most of the flower paintings which Bierk uses were painted by Manet or by Fantin-Latour, whose work he saw in an exhibition at the National Gallery of Canada. In many cultures, including our own, flowers are given as an offering and tribute to someone, to a memory, to a hero. Bierk's gesture of placing the flowers next to fragments from old master works is as personal and touching a dedication as that made by the Boston collector Isabella Stewart Gardiner, who had her own greenhouse built with her museum so that carefully co-ordinated flower arrangements could be put before some of her favorite paintings. Louise Lawler notes that the museum today uses flowers made of silk. Bierk's floral still-lifes are a far cry from a faded reproduction. They are painted with an exuberant affirmation of life.

The questions most often asked about Bierk's work concern themselves with the artist's choice of images. Is the reason for painting a Manet flower the remaking of a commodity which is out of most people's reach because of the escalated world market for masterpieces? Why are no such masterpieces in Peterborough? Could it be a desire Bierk shares with Manet to make a link with the art of the past as reference, as model, as emulating a superior time in art production, or to break through the borders of nationality? In order to make his juxtapositions, Bierk could simply have used a photo reproduction of Manet's flowers and collaged it into his work. But photo reproductions are like photographs in that they are a record of what is past, whereas painting is in the present. The act of painting Manet's flowers transforms the reproduction into a plausible representation in the present. The painting is an actual primary reality painted more in the sense of 'after' Manet than 'of' a Manet. In these works David Bierk never disguises his own vigorous brushstroke. Even when the work is based on his own photographs, Bierk is not satisfied with the surface of the photograph itself, but paints over it and into it, negating the photograph's presence and changing its landscape to paint. In some recent work, Bierk cuts the photo's delicate skin, again changing that secondary reality into a primary one scored with his personal mark.

In the painting *A Eulogy to Art, David Watching, to Fantin-Latour*, 1990, the left panel depicts a Fantin-Latour flower piece set under glass in one of Bierk's typical painted plaster 'walls'. The panel on the right is an enlarged photograph of seven men carrying a large painting through the streets of Florence, probably a painting damaged in the flood. The photographer who recorded the scene placed himself at a high vantage point above Michelangelo's statue of David, who ends up 'watching' the procession below. 'As Marshall McLuhan pointed out in the 1960s, nothing is so bizarre as the juxtapositions that occur everyday on the front page of a good newspaper, and the Post-Modern sensibility has been subjected to even greater incongruity by television'.[7] In this work Bierk's source is a newspaper photograph which he has enlarged and delicately tinted. No doubt the original image was placed in the newspaper to draw our attention to the fragile nature of our artistic treasures, and the photographer who recorded the event felt the excitement of incongruous juxtapositions.

Bierk, on viewing the image, immediately tuned in to its potential. He says in the title that this work is a eulogy to art. The word 'eulogy' carries the double connotation of being a funeral speech, but could also be simply words of praise. For an artist like Bierk, the joy of painting images by old masters is definitely done in the spirit of praise, in celebration and as an homage to the act of painting. Although Bierk embraces the present with such enthusiasm, there are always messages, even warnings. David Bierk will never be a painter of simple objects because he always carries a loaded brush.

A Eulogy to Art, David Watching,
to Fantin-Latour
oil on canvas, oil on
plaster on plywood,
oil on photo
54" x 138"
1989
Collection: Art Gallery of Peterborough,
Peterborough, Ont.

REFERENCES

1   André Malraux, *The Voices of Silence, Museum Without Walls*, translated from the French by Stuart Gilbert and Francis Price,
    Doubleday & Company, Inc., Garden City, New York, 1967.

2   Charles Baudelaire, *Art In Paris 1845-1862, Salons and Exhibitions*, translated and edited by Jonathan Mayne, Phaidon Press, 1965, p. 154.

3   Douglas Crimp, 'On the Museum's Ruins', *The Anti-Aesthetic, Essays on Postmodern Culture*, edited and with an introduction by Hal Foster,
    Bay Press, Port Townsend, Washington, 1983, p. 53.

4   Rosalind Krauss, 'A Note on Photography and the Simulacral', *October*, Nr. 31, Winter 1984, p. 56.

5   Michael Fried, 'Manet's Sources, Aspects of his Art, 1859-1865', *Artforum*, March, 1969, pp. 28-82.

6   Trevor Fairbrother, Acting Curator of Contemporary Art, Contemporary Art at the Museum of Fine Arts, Boston, *Connections: Louise Lawler*,
    November 17, 1990-March 3, 1991, exhibition brochure.

7   Charles Jencks, *What is Post-Modernism?*, Academy Editions/St.Martin's Press, New York, 1987, p. 55.

Parable of Existence,
to Claude Lorrain
oil on plaster, plywood and steel
43" x 22"
1993

A PORTRAIT

Self-portrait
oil on canvas
6' diameter
1970

by Dennis Tourbin

We were at the Memorial Centre,
David Bierk, Billy the K and I,
watching the fights: Sugar Ray
Leonard and Thomas Hit Man Hearns.
It was a big fight on closed
circuit and we had ringside
seats. It was Rock-a-Billy's idea.
And we were all there drinking beer
and watching big screen TV and David
asked me if I would write a piece
for the catalogue of his one-man
exhibition which would be touring
Ontario. It was then that he asked
me if I would write this that I am
writing right now.

I first met David Bierk in his studio
at 408½ George St. N. near the old
Mardi Gras Dance Studio, in the
building that Meyer Levine owned.
Meyer had a special understanding
of artists, I don't know why,
he just did. I had been talking
with John Boyle on the phone a
few days before I first met David.

John told me that he had met an
artist from Peterborough by the
name of David Bierk and wanted to
know if I had met him yet. I told
him that I hadn't met him, not yet.
John said that he had and that he did,
David did large spray paintings. John
said that I should keep my eye open
for him.

■ Rock-a-Billy Kimball

■ Meyer Levine, friend, landlord and critic – daily – for 20 years

■ David with fold installation at the Art Gallery of Peterborough, 1981

I remember my first meeting with David;
it was on the 3rd floor of Meyer's
building above Hair Care on George St.,
as I said before. We sat in green
metal lawn chairs in his studio and
we talked. We talked about dreams,
contemporary dreams. We agreed that
art was larger than life and that
Peterborough was but a stop on the way.
We both looked forward to the day when
our art would go beyond Peterborough
and be visible to a much larger
public. We discovered that we
had many things in common.

■ David dwarfed by one of his rock paintings, 1978

■ Dennis Tourbin, John Boyle and David at the original *Artspace* on Water Street, 1975

A few days later I visited David
again at his studio. His young son
Sebastian was reading an article from
artscanada to him as he painted. I
forget the title of the painting but
I can see it clearly in my mind right
now at this moment. Sebastian was
reading art history to David while
David was painting. That is a
firm memory in my mind …
David set his brush down.
Sebastian stopped reading
and David smiled, completely
aware of the realism, completely
aware of the moment. And we
talked for the longest time, or
for what seemed like the longest
time.

■ *A Shared Dream …* (in progress)

■ Source photograph for *A Shared Dream …*,
taken in the Bahamas, 1971

■ Final version:

A Shared Dream, Homage to Henri Rousseau, The Canadian Indian, Charlie Brown, Leonardo da Vinci,
Larry Poons, Larry Gray, The California Grape and Fine Art in General, oil on canvas, 8½' x 9', 1975
Collection: S. Bierk, New Jersey

And from that moment on we became
good friends, dear friends, and
whenever I was in Peterborough
I would visit him at his studio and
when I wasn't in Peterborough we
would talk on the telephone. We
both liked talking on the telephone.
And sometimes we would talk for hours.

A telephone is as important as a
paint brush to a modern artist and
with David Bierk this is especially
true. He will call anywhere in the
world at the drop of a hat to get the
information he needs. Why waste time.

So anyway, as I said, sometimes we would
talk for hours on the telephone, making
plans for exhibitions, discussing new
ideas, trying to discover a balance
in our lives which would allow the
creative spirit an opportunity not
only to survive, but to flourish.

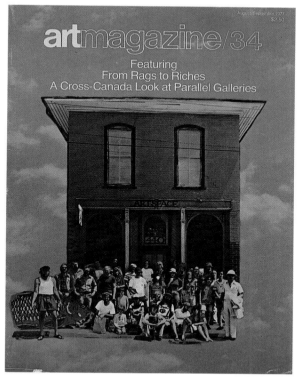

■ *Artspace* and artists on the cover of *artmagazine*, 1977

■ Dennis Tourbin and David at *Artspace*, 1975

■ 'Monument to Miniature' exhibition at the Market Hall, Peterborough, 1975

Nothing seemed impossible to David, whether it was the immense dimensions of a huge painting that he happened to want to create or whether it was the creation of a contemporary art centre run completely by artists that he felt was so important for the artists and the community that he lived in. Nothing seemed impossible to David.

He challenged us with his ideas about art and about politics. He approached everything with a spontaneous exuberance, a reckless abandon. I remember once, a year or so ago, I was at home painting in my studio and the telephone rang. It was David. He was laughing. He was absolutely giddy with laughter, so much so that it was impossible for him to speak. Well, of course I started to laugh too. And there we were, the two of us laughing our heads off on the telephone and I didn't even know why, until finally he said, 'Guess who I have just been talking to for the past hour?' Well, I had absolutely no idea and I told him so. 'Christo,' David said.
'Who?' I said.
'Christo, you know, the guy who did the running fence in California, the modern-day da Vinci.'

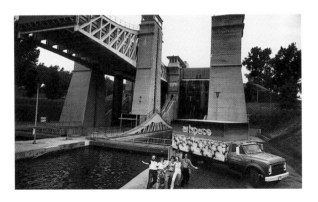

■ *Artspace* staff and the award-winning truck, 'Big Blue', at the Peterborough Liftlocks, 1979

■ Preparing for the 'Christo' exhibition, *Artspace* on Hunter Street, 1981

■ Christo at *Artspace* with his work, *Wrapped Walkways*, 1981

There was absolute silence on the
telephone. I was stunned.
'He's coming to Peterborough and
installing an exhibition at Artspace.
Do you believe that?' said David.
I asked him how he could possibly have
arranged that and he said, 'I just
picked up the telephone and called him.'
'Where did you ever get the number?'
I asked. 'I just called New York
information, got the number and
called him,' replied David.
'Isn't that amazing!'

Well, it is amazing, or it was amazing.
Over the years I have learned to expect
the unexpected from David. There is
no limit to his possibilities. Give
him a project and a deadline and he
will arrive on time against all odds.
That is the way David is.

David is an artist and an arts
administrator; that is a difficult
job for anyone at the best of times
and David is certainly no exception
to the rule. He does, however, have
the advantage of working with Liz
Bierk and she has provided the kind of
enthusiasm and spirit, the sheer hard
work and determination which have been
absolutely necessary for David to
handle the two jobs effectively.

■ David 'doing business' in his George Street studio, Peterborough, 1993

■ Liz Bierk, wife and partner for 13 years, 1993

But in spite of Liz's involvement
in David's career there are still times
when David has questioned the amount
of time and energy he has put into
the administrative end rather than
the creative end of his art.

I remember once just before a board
meeting at Artspace a few years ago,
a time when things were very hectic
at Artspace and David was in a
particularly low mood. David wasn't
often in a low mood but this time
was an exception. I think we were
preparing for the 'Reflecting A
Rural Consciousness' exhibition
in Paris, France. Anyway, David
was talking to Ian McLachlan prior
to the meeting and he happened to
wonder aloud about all of the paintings
he hadn't painted because of his intense
involvement with Artspace …
Ian seemed surprised by this and said,
'But David, Artspace is probably one
of the greatest works of art that
you have created.'

■ David and Liz with Badanna Zack's cow, 'Reflecting A Rural Consciousness'
exhibition, 1981

■ Paterson Ewen and Ian McLachlan at David's studio, 1985

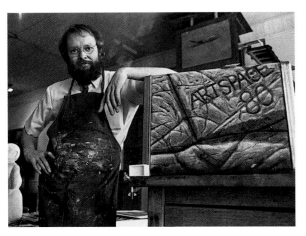

■ David with the famous 'Artspace suitcase', 1985

David thought about it for a moment and then he smiled. He understood what Ian had said. And I don't want this to be misunderstood because we all know that there were many, many people involved in the creation of Artspace, but it was David Bierk and his single-minded determination that really brought Artspace to life. The development of Artspace is a very clear example of his keen sense of community, his dedication to artists and ideas and his willingness to put words into action.

But Artspace is only one side of David. There is still the other side – the artist, the painter. In many ways David is very much a traditionalist. He knows that in spite of the electronic revolution painting will never disappear. Painting belongs to nature.

I have watched David's painting develop over the past ten years and I have witnessed what I think is quite a remarkable development, from Shirley Temple to family portraits, from paintings of friends to the cremation of Sam McGee, a work which became a Canadian stamp. David has continually strived to discover something new and exciting in his painting.

■ *Self-portrait*, 1972

■ *Friends Series*, 1982

■ *Sam McGee* stamp commission, 1975

I remember when he had finished the huge portrait of the Queen for the Memorial Centre in Peterborough. I watched as David supervised the installation. Members of the Petes hockey team were skating around on the ice and a few people were sitting in the stands. As the large painting was hoisted up to the position high in the rafters I remember noticing as I watched the painting being raised that it did not diminish in size in my eye. The portrait maintained that important physical presence which is so important in painting today.

One has only to look at the complex dimensionality of Bierk's newest works, the folds, or at the stark beautiful realism of his rocks to realize that one is looking at the work of a truly gifted and fine creative artist.

■ David preparing his *Portrait of Queen Elizabeth II* moments before its installation in the Peterborough Memorial Centre, 1984

Right:

IT'S JUST A MATTER OF TASTE, EH?

An icon for Canadian unity, dedicated to Claude Monet, Vincent van Gogh, Maxfield Parrish, Caspar David Friedrich, Larry Gray, Tom Thomson, the Ant Farm, Sir Lawrence Alma Tadema, the Peterborough Liftlocks, well designed cars, transportation, dreams and communication through art; A proposal to give John Bentley Mays the Chateau Lake Louise to form a Canadian school of criticism; The dolphins are named Video, Performance Art, Constructivism, Formal Abstraction and Lyrical Expressionism; A political party once suggested moving the Rocky Mountains to Quebec City as an incentive for Canadian Unity; Art has no borders, no limits, and the words on paper and the images on the wall are only meanings within you; And I wonder how many national treasures might have been seen if Air Canada, Canadian National and Canadian Pacific were the National Gallery, instead of the thousands of paintings rotting away in a basement seen by none; And where is the shock of the new; And where is Vuillard; Victor Coleman should run the Canada Council, not a theatre; Forget regionalism and go global and beyond; And I am sad and angry when I drive down Lansdowne Street and think I am in L.A.

mixed media

6' x 14'

1981

Collection: The Canada Council Art Bank, Ottawa, Ont.

■ In the studio, 1993

A CONVERSATION

DENNIS TOURBIN WITH DAVID BIERK

■ The first *Artspace*, Water St.

■ *Artspace* opening, Ray Woodworth
(centre)

DENNIS TOURBIN : I'd like to begin by asking you about Artspace. When I returned from France just at the end of 1982 Artspace was at 190 Hunter Street. What motivated the desire to get out of there?

DAVID BIERK : Very similarly to when Artspace moved from its first home at 440 Water Street, it just seemed that we had … I wouldn't say outgrown the facilities, but we had reached a limit to what it was possible to do within that space. The other thing was that when we originally moved into the Hunter Street space we had a very good deal on rent, but five years down the road we were subject to a rent review when interest rates were very, very high, and mortgage rates were high and so our rent was to be doubled. We simply said that if our rent was going to go from $450 to $900 a month we could do better, and maybe get a larger space.

DT : I remember there were a lot of people coming in and out of Artspace because it had become such a centre not only of the visual arts but also of performance art events, poetry, and music.

DB : Absolutely. When I think back to the original location at 440 Water Street it sometimes seems as if it was a one or two person operation. Then at 190 Hunter Street it was as if everything was working on all cylinders, and you had whole groups of people working in theatre, working in music, working in dance. Poetry was almost a full-time program. I can remember going to ANNPAC – the umbrella organization for artist-run centres – meetings and talking about turn-away crowds to your own readings at Artspace, Dennis, and that was simply unheard-of. When you look back at how the parallel galleries had evolved to that point and since then, we were probably the first large general artist-run centre. In Toronto at that time you had 15 Dance Lab, Music Gallery, A Space – all with very specific mandates and programs, whereas Artspace, because it was in Peterborough and because there weren't a lot of other people working in those disciplines, had it all happening under one roof. We were being pushed to our limits and we simply had to – even when we took over the ground floor and and went from a one floor operation to a two floor operation – we just had to expand.

DT : It seemed to me that Artspace was very accessible to people, people felt comfortable going there – the students from Trent University and Sir Sandford Fleming College, the members of the contemporary cultural community – and found in Artspace a place where many of their creative needs could be explored. It was comfortable for people to work there.

DB : Absolutely.

DT : The decision to move away from that situation with Artspace must have been very difficult.

DB : I can remember making trips to the United States and to Europe and seeing the emphasis that was placed on contemporary art, and then coming back to Canada and thinking that we in the artist-run centre network were somehow ghettoized, living some kind of third world existence. Why should art always be up

■ David, Hunter St. *Artspace*

■ ANNPAC meeting, late '70s: Glenn Lewis, Clive Robertson, Toby Anderson, Trevor Goring, John Oswald,
Lawrence Adams, David Bierk, Dennis Tourbin, Marien Lewis, Brenda Wallace, René Blouin and others

■ The Market Hall tower

■ David, Dennis and the work crew in the Market Hall

a flight of stairs or in a basement? Why should you always struggle with very, very minimal staff and budgets? Why should it be four blocks out of the core of the city? The whole idea of the move to the Market Hall was – if nothing else – a very bold experiment, so why not take it a step further?

DT : So you zeroed in on the Market Hall, which is a large, beautiful space right in the heart of Peterborough. Describe how you went about getting the Market Hall.

DB : There are so many wonderful stories attached to that move. One of the very first exhibitions that Artspace did while still under the roof at 440 Water Street was the 'Monument to Miniature' exhibition in the early seventies …

DT : Which was in the Market Hall?

DB : Which was in the Market Hall before it had been developed. It was like a huge, open, condemned space.

DT : And it was vacant for years after that exhibition?

DB : Yes. If you look at the whole history of the Market Hall, it was the place where, for the last century, farmers from in and around Peterborough would bring their produce to sell. It was a market and it was a very public place in the heart of the city on the corner of George St. and Charlotte St., the equivalent of Yonge and Bloor in Toronto, I suppose – an incredible space. It was the obvious place for an arts centre.

DT : Who owned it then?

DB : It was owned by Marathon Realty. We had to raise one and a half million dollars to move into that space, deal with a work crew of over thirty, and engineers, architects and city planners. Yet the hardest hurdle to get over was Marathon Realty, because we were talking about a state of the art, alternative cultural centre – theatre, gallery, recording facilities – in the city's most historically significant nineteenth-century commercial building, a space that always had incredible potential but no

■ Francis Fox and Barry McDougall, MPP, with the Market Hall model

viable use. It had forty-four foot high ceilings, ten thousand square feet, a cavernous open space that Peterborough Square, which occupied the ground floor, could never fit a steak house or offices or twenty-two shoe stores into or whatever … When we went to Marathon with our idea, they were used to dealing with people who wanted a two-year commercial lease. We went to them and said if we can get money from the Department of Communications and the Ministry of Culture and Recreation in Ontario they're going to want a minimum twenty-year lease. They're not going to pour a million dollars into this place and have the lease expire in two years. It was like trying to mix oil and water. It seemed impossible. I thought we could persuade them by actually showing them what we wanted to do. And so in typical Artspace fashion, with no budget, we got an old piece of plywood, cut it up, put it together and made our own architectural 'model' that we were very proud of. The roof came off and inside we had made false walls, walls on wheels, little paintings on all the panels, a sound booth, and stages …

DT : I remember it looked terrific.

DB : Yes. But to take that model, with me in my three-piece blue suit, to … I don't know … the twenty-second floor of the Marathon building on Bay Street in Toronto and simply walk in, it was amazing. My wife Liz and I had an appointment but got there a little early and met the receptionist as we lugged this grey box, which looked a bit like a dog house from the outside. We were ushered down a hall with the thickest carpets I've ever walked on into a room the size of a gallery, beautifully lit, beautifully detailed, and there were models of projects all over the room, all of the Marathon projects that were on the go all over the world, in Rio de Janeiro, San Francisco, Vancouver, Toronto – the models themselves, I'm sure, cost more than our entire project … kinetic things, lights, glass, movable things. And there was our grey plywood box. It was too much!

DT : So how did Marathon respond in the end?

DB : Well, the Marathon man we dealt with, Jim Butler, loved the concept and believed in us and the project enough to take up the challenge, help us through the enormous number of meetings and legal wranglings that it took to strike a deal, a very good deal – five dollars a year in rent for twenty years for the Market Hall. Jim was one of our strongest allies, and his support and the Marathon offer were the key to the rest of the monies we required falling into place.

DT : Did the City of Peterborough support the idea at the time?

DB : Well, I think the City was very cautious in the beginning, but definitely hopeful.

DT : Artspace had a track record of success.

DB : Yes, but Artspace was alternative. As often as not there was controversy attached to any of Artspace's major successes. For instance, everybody loved it when we brought Christo to Peterborough. Seven hundred people came to hear him talk, art students were bused in from Toronto, and the mayor introduced him and presented him with a City of Peterborough plate – it was a whirlwind art event! Then there was the Canadian Images Film Festival. Artspace showed a censored film and all of a sudden three of us – Ian McLachlan, Susan Ditta and I – were in court fighting the Ontario censorship laws. There was always controversy. I don't think we could have the same success now. Can you imagine a city and a huge corporation like Marathon letting a group of artists take on a project of that scale?

■ Ribbon cutting, Market Hall opening: David, Dennis, Mayor Barker, Jon Hobbs, Gary Joffre-Clark, Liz, Bill Kimball (kneeling)

■ Above, centre: Work crew and officials at announcement of the Market Hall project funding by the Department of Communications

DT : I agree it would be very difficult to imagine it happening now. One of the things I found most exciting about that situation is that at a point in time when everybody was being cautious, when people weren't spending money on projects, the artists moved in, into the heart of the city and provided employment for part of the population in Peterborough. It was a remarkable project.

DB : Well, absolutely. And at that phase …

DT : The artists took the chance.

DB : Yes. Then the city got behind the project. There were editorials in the *Examiner* calling it the most important renovation project to happen in downtown Peterborough in a decade. The city certainly became very excited by that, and the citizenry as well. Yet, unlike the Art Gallery of Peterborough or the Museum, we had to go out and raise all of that money ourselves. When they did projects, it was assumed that because they were under the city wing their projects would be funded.

DT : Who designed the space?

DB : It was my design, at least my conceptual design. Then a good friend in Ottawa, Stefan Hensel, an architect, came and walked through the Market Hall with me, let me dream out loud and imagine a stage here and a bank of offices there, a control bridge and walls on wheels so that everything was portable, everything was flexible. Stefan was so inspired that he went back to Ottawa and three days later a tube arrived with six full pages of architectural details! And it was there, there it was on paper. From that point on Jon Hobbs, a local architect, and a marvelous contractor, Gary Joffre-Clark, were both involved in the project.

DT : What about the work crew?

DB : Fortunately, we qualified for employment projects whereby we could get government money to take people off unemployment and recruit people in retraining programs. Also, Sir Sandford Fleming College had programs we were able to tap into. It was a real community effort. We simply worked with what we had.

DT : At the same time Artspace was still doing programming out of your studio.

DB : That's right. We also did 'satellite' programmes in places like Peter Robinson College at Trent University and even sometimes in storefronts. We kept our programming going during the entire time. I felt very strongly that this was important.

DT : That's pretty remarkable. Other places would probably have suspended programming during the building phase. Artspace didn't.

DB : Dennis, when I remember what we did all those years it still amazes me, and you were such a very, very important part of it. What you just said about other spaces not taking the chance that we did is something I can relate to. We took an exhibition to Paris, France on about one month's notice. You coined the phrases 'reckless abandon' and 'racing to the moon'. Artspace never was just a building or four walls – it's not now and I hope it never will be. It was the spirit that said you could determine your own destiny. We came to Peterborough at a time when nothing like this existed, when there was still money available from the councils to do things, to build things, to dream things. I think we were very – well, luck had nothing to do with it, but maybe fate did.

DT : A large part has to do with you, your leadership, your drive and your ambition not to accept something that just wasn't right. Certainly the move to the Market Hall was one of the most excit-

■ Market Hall opening: David, Jim Butler, Dennis Tourbin, Mayor Barker, Jon Hobbs, Gary Joffre-Clark, Liz, Bill Kimball, Alex and Jeff Bierk (foreground)

■ Mark Prent

■ Installation: Vera Frenkel at *Artspace*

■ Dorothy Caldwell at the 'Architectural Paper' exhibition

ing times for the artists of this community, and it succeeded. At the same time that was going on, your own work had to proceed and develop.

DB : Being at Artspace was never a job, it was always an extension of my art or, as you called it once, 'a conceptual Meccano set'. To create such a place provided a direct link to one's art. It was always a very, very creative experience. During those thirteen years at Artspace I was painting, exhibiting, getting the odd grant and trying my very best to do good work. But like every other Canadian artist I knew then, I had to depend upon things like Artspace and teaching and projects, not my painting, as my primary source of income. Once the Market Hall was built and operational, six months later I felt that I needed a break. I asked the board for a 'sabbatical', essentially to paint and still be there if needed, but really just to take a break from it.

DT : One of the things that often happens in this kind of situation is that there is an incredible sense of development, a building process which requires an awful lot of stamina, courage and faith. In the end there is a need to step back, a need to rejuvenate oneself. Yet unfortunately there isn't a financial structure within the system to provide for this need.

DB : It was very scary for me because, quite frankly, Artspace was doing very well. It had a complete, talented staff of people and the budget was around three hundred thousand dollars a year. My frustration was that in order to raise the amount of money necessary to keep everything going at this level, I had to spend far more time fundraising than working with artists, putting up exhibitions, writing a catalogue or whatever.

DT : One thing I want to mention is that when one thinks of Artspace and the work that you have done there, it's easy to forget the great programming which came from you, amazing exhibitions, going back as far as 'Monument to Miniature', 'Reflecting A Rural Consciousness', 'Rags to Riches' – and I'm only talking about the local exhibitions that you put together that really challenged artists to create work in new and different ways. You also brought in Michael Snow, Paterson Ewen …

■ Paul Wong

■ Margaret Dragu

■ Marien Lewis

DB : Noel Harding, Christo, Mark Prent. Artspace became well known on a national level at that time, and with the move to the Market Hall I would say that it was pushing an international reputation. After the great effort it took – two years in construction – actually to build the facility we had thought about for so long, we took tremendous pride in every single exhibition. We painted all the walls brick red and marbleized the baseboards for 'The Romantic Landscape Now' and then repainted them for 'Architectural Paper', some of these really major installations. Then high school kids would come in the next week and we'd give the kids' exhibitions the same care and treatment we had given the international stars … It was wonderful.

DT : The equivalent would be a high school hockey team playing in Maple Leaf Gardens.

DB : [*Laughing*] Yes. I can remember coming into Artspace during the second month after we were open in the Market Hall, having been away for a few days, and walking through the offices and seeing these new typewriters that we had cranking out fundraising letters. Next, I walked through the 'Architectural Paper' show. We had, as you say, artists living out their dreams in this space with art that literally filled the forty-four foot high ceilings. I went into the theatre behind the gallery – this was at two o'clock in the afternoon – and saw probably four hundred people in that theatre listening to Noam Chomsky speak on human rights atrocities in East Timor. It was simply unbelievable to see everything actually working, that in the visual arts area there was an incredible exhibition, and then the enormous audience at the lecture. The place we had built was actually working and I was standing back and witnessing it all.

DT : It wasn't the same place, though, was it, David?

DB : No. It never is. When you move from somewhere to get to

■ Michael Snow

■ Installation: 'The Physicality of Landscape' (Paterson Ewen, Christo, Marlene Creates), *Artspace*, 1986

■ Installation: John Boyle, Dennis Tourbin, Dorothy Caldwell, *Artspace*, 1987

a new place you leave the old place. You see, we dreamed about it in the late seventies. We got serious about it and then built it in the early eighties, and then as the economic situation evolved to where it is now in the early nineties, what was possible then has become very difficult now. But my career has taken me to other places and I'm very happy to be where I am now, and quite frankly after the sabbatical I never looked back. I view Artspace as thirteen incredible years of my life, very significant and very, very satisfying. Now that focus, energy and determination have been applied to my own work. Artspace is still there and the fact that it has survived throughout these years is a testimony to its original concept and the efforts of many people who have contributed to its programmes over the years. It continues to embrace artists, academics and the general public, a really broad audience.

DT : I agree. The quiet satisfaction of knowing that one played a part is something that a lot of people in Peterborough and beyond can be very proud of.

DB : Exactly. When we first met each other in Peterborough, this place was new and obviously different from Toronto and California, but there was this love of place which we both felt and the undeniable challenge to make it work. I think that artists more than other people have got to contribute to the situation in order for it to improve. I'm very, very proud of those years and of what we built. I get a lot of satisfaction when reading in the paper about how often Artspace is used. The public is really using it.

DT : When you left Artspace you immersed yourself in your work as I had never seen before and the results were quite obvious. You produced an amazing body of work and … well, you tell me what happened.

DB : I learned a lot from being on the receiving side of the desk at Artspace. I made a point of knowing what was going on in contemporary art in general, not only in Canada but in the United States and Europe. I learned a lot about 'the system'. What I wanted to do more than anything else was paint. So basically I decided that during my six months' leave I wanted to produce a body of work and at the same time find a place to exhibit within the commercial gallery system. I knew that this would be the only way to support myself and my family.

DT : Did you have a team of people working in your studio at that time, or were you working alone?

DB : No, no. Totally by myself. I knew the timing was right. When I was going to the California College of Arts & Crafts doing realistic painting, abstract expressionism was the only thing being thought about, being discussed, being taught in school. I was against the grain. During the seventies and eighties when I was doing historical images, appropriating art history, before appropriation was a word in the art vocabulary, I was against the grain. But all of a sudden in 1984, when I took this leave of absence to go to New York and Los Angeles, my work fit within a validated contemporary mainstream.

DT : You had a body of work?

DB : I had not only a body of work but an eighteen-year history behind it.

DT : Where did you go?

DB : I went first to New York and found an affordable hotel and said to myself that I was going to spend three days going to every single important gallery in New York City.

DT : Just to look?

DB : I wanted to look and I wanted to evaluate and I wanted to try to figure out if I fit and …

DT : What did you do?

DB : During the first two days I went to, I think, one hundred and fifty-seven galleries and short-listed the twenty or thirty which I was interested in, or galleries which I thought might be interested in my work. Actually, I did that in a day and a half. The second day and a half I spent going back to those places with a binder of slides. In every case I would simply introduce myself, say that I was from Canada, that I was going to California in two days, and could somebody look at the slides. On average one out of every five would say yes and four would say they could not look at them at the moment. But the minute one person ended up being interested and opened up the binder I knew that somehow I had cracked the most difficult part of the process. Once they saw my work – the photography was a major part of the work, landscapes, painted photographs – I have to say they were very interested.

DT : Did you get a dealer in New York?

DB : No, but I came away from New York with very sincere interest in my work on the part of two or three galleries, some very good galleries.

DT : When you left New York did you know in which ones you wanted to exhibit?

DB : No, but I had this great feeling of confidence because everybody who looked at my work liked it, or at least respected it. I knew that it could hold its own in the centre of the North American art world.

DT : Next you went to Los Angeles?

DB : Yes. I had two days in L.A. and there were fewer galleries much more spread out, geographically speaking. It was a different kind of task, but again the same approach. I had a copy of *Artforum* with a full-page ad for the Jan Turner Gallery and it showed a romantic landscape and I thought, 'Well, here's a great place to start,' because I was doing romantic landscapes at that time. I was convinced that my work was as good as if not better than the painting in the ad, and I had heard of the Jan Turner Gallery. So, at nine-thirty in the morning, before the gallery was even open, I arrived with my slides – and I'll never ever forget this experience. I walked in and saw the exhibition by the artist in the ad, Bruce Everett – large scale, romantic landscape paintings. I just had this feeling that somehow this might be the place for me. I loved the space.

■ Jan Turner

DT : You had to get by the desk, right?

DB : Yes, I had to get by the desk knowing that these people get twenty artists a day asking the same question and they don't always have time to deal with you. My approach was an open and honest one. I remember encountering the very attractive woman sitting behind the desk, thinking she was probably a student. Later I found out that she, Deborah, became the director of the prestigious Blum Helman Gallery, and then head of contemporary art for Christies in Beverly Hills. Getting through her to Jan Turner was actually a very formidable task. I explained my situation to her and said, 'Look, I'd just really like to show the work to Jan Turner – is there any way?' She said, 'I'm sorry, Jan Turner is leaving for New York tomorrow, she has a ton of stuff to do and there's just no way … ' But she was very helpful in pointing out some other galleries that I should see while I was in Los Angeles. That day I probably saw about sixty or seventy galleries and again created a short list and again had my next day planned. Also, I thought I would go back to Jan Turner and just see if there was any way she would see me – just in case. Of all the places I had seen in New York and L.A., her gallery was the one I liked the best. I went back and there was Deborah sitting behind the desk and I walked up to her again and said, 'Look, I went to one hundred and fifty galleries in New York, I went to seventy galleries today. This is my favourite. I'm going to leave this binder here with the hope that Jan Turner will walk by tonight and take it home with her to have a look at it. Can I do that?' She agreed. By now she kind of liked me, or at least she thought I was a pretty gutsy Canadian. I went back at ten o'clock the next morning and remember opening the door, looking at Deborah behind the desk and her giving me the 'thumbs down'. Obviously Jan Turner had not seen the the binder. I picked it up and said, 'Look, thank you very much for trying, but I am going to mail this to you and I hope you remember me when it arrives. Thank you very much.' As I walked towards the door she said, 'Wait a minute. Jan's in there right now. Give me the binder and I'll get it to her. I can tell you it's a one in ten shot, but I'll do it.' I wandered out into the Bruce Everett exhibition and looked at it for the third time. About ten minutes went by and I was thinking, 'Oh God, she doesn't have time. I should get out of here.' And I turned around and a woman walked towards me and introduced herself as Jan Turner. And she proceeded to tell me that she liked my work very much, she

■ Installation: Jan Turner Gallery, Los Angeles, Calif.

wanted to talk to me and she had just delayed her flight to New York. We sat down and talked for two hours about art, life, family, television, Hollywood, Minnesota, Canada, Peterborough, Artspace – everything. It was one of those incredible occasions where you meet a person who is in tune with your thoughts and ideas. And that was it! At the end of the conversation she said, 'I want to represent you in Los Angeles.'

DT : Was this a well established gallery, David, or a relatively new gallery?

DB : She had been in the business for seventeen years. It was a beautiful place on Melrose Avenue with a wonderful staff of people, wonderful art – it was perfect. I couldn't believe it. After painting for twenty years, after plugging away at Artspace, and after hearing how this sort of thing happens to some people but for some reason it hasn't happened to you … I've been a teacher, I've been an administrator, I live in Peterborough – there are all these things you think are against you – but somehow you still hope that with perseverance somewhere down the road something will happen, someone will give you a chance. After our meeting, I walked out the door onto Melrose Avenue and let out the largest 'whooop' you've ever heard and realized that they probably heard me inside the gallery. Three years later, after an opening there, Jan took my wife and me out to dinner and she told us how incredible it was that I had come out of nowhere, because she had never taken artists on without knowing their work for at least a few years and never done on the strength of slides alone, but that in my case something happened and she said yes. When they heard the 'whooop' they all went out to the door thinking something had happened to me, that I had been mugged or something! Jan also said I did the funniest thing she had ever seen in her life: I walked to my car, which was about a half a block away, and just before I got to it I jumped right up into the air and clicked my heels *à la* Gene Kelly!

DT : But David, Los Angeles, California is an awfully long way from Peterborough, Ontario.

DB : Jan thought the L.A. Art Fair – a month away! – would be the way to introduce my work to California. It was agreed that I would try to finish six or eight landscape paintings that I was working on and have them framed for the Fair. How could I say no? Have you ever known me to say no?

DT : [*Laughing*] You finally shipped them down to L.A.?

DB : When I got back to Peterborough, I finished the paintings, had them framed, built a crate and they were off. The paintings did sell at the fair. It was the beginning of a whole new way of doing things.

DT : Did you have a dealer in Toronto at that time?

DB : No.

DT : Any thought of approaching one?

DB : Toronto dealers had known what I was doing during all my Artspace years. I had an experience in 1975 with Nancy Poole which for me was the kind of thorn in my side that pushed me a little harder to make Artspace succeed.

DT : Nancy Poole's Studio?

DB : Yes, it was a very good gallery in Yorkville. I had one successful show there in 1975 and another one in 1976. In that year the rent had doubled and the increase was passed on to the artists. The second year I had to pay seven hundred and fifty dollars just to exhibit. I had to pay for the announcements. I had to pay for transportation. If I wanted the work insured I had to pay for that too.

On top of it there was a fifty percent commission! It was this situation that motivated me to make Artspace work – I felt there had to be an alternative to the system, that you could determine your own destiny, that you could do something on your own. Still, thirteen years after the Nancy Poole episode, I realized that if I really wanted to do what I wanted to do, which was paint, then I had to link into the commercial gallery network and find the best dealers and the best markets that would enable me to stay in Peterborough and do it.

DT : So you had Los Angeles …

DB : Los Angeles was the first one, and then I started showing my work with the Diane Farris Gallery in Vancouver. At the same time I made a very serious pitch to the Wynick/Tuck Gallery in Toronto. Throughout my time at Artspace I'd kept in touch with Lynne Wynick and David Tuck, showing them slides of my work on a regular basis. But there was a reluctance by other Toronto dealers to take on my work because it never fit into the heart of any Toronto mainstream. To me, Toronto was always too sensitive to New York or to whatever was the mainstream in New York or Europe, and my work was certainly against that grain. My work is very emotional and passionate and very much about beauty and painting, things which were the antithesis of much of that Toronto scene.

DT : When did your final approach to the Wynick/Tuck Gallery happen?

DB : They had seen my show in 1981 at the Art Gallery of

■ Installation: Wynick/Tuck Gallery, Toronto, Ont.

• The studio visit during which we came to offer representation to David is one of those experiences that every dealer hopes for but are far too infrequent.

We had been aware of David and his work for more than a decade. David would appear in our gallery every year or two, slides in hand, asking if we'd like to have a look. He was an active exhibitor in parallel and public galleries, and often would have an exhibition announcement, or even a catalogue, as well. The work was always engaging, but it was more his innate enthusiasm, positive outlook and obvious commitment to what he was doing both in his artwork and with Artspace that persuaded us to make the trek all the way up to Peterborough on more than one occasion. Usually these trips were tied in with one or another exhibition at Artspace or the Art Gallery of Peterborough, but there was always a studio visit.

Although we had always liked and respected David's work, we continued to conclude that there was some small intangible missing from it that prevented us from feeling entirely comfortable that it was appropriate for our gallery's specific audience.

The final visit, in the spring of 1987, found Lynne and me driving north on a day that, with the heat and humidity, could have been one of the most unpleasant in the depths of a muggy Toronto summer. Perhaps that contributed to our mutual grumblings about why were doing this yet again.

At that time, David had been on sabbatical for about six months, relatively free from the concerns of Artspace and painting full time. When we walked into his studio there were a number of works stacked against the walls as well as several works from the past few months of painting that David had selected to hang.

We were immediately struck by these and knew instantly that whatever intangible we felt had been missing before was not missing now. On the contrary, all of the ideas he had been dealing with, both visually and conceptually, for some time had gelled into very exciting, well-conceived works. We sent David off into a back room in search of some earlier work (mostly so we could talk together) and agreed on the spot that we should take him on. However, to make sure these particular works were not just a lucky fluke of some kind, we looked at all of the rest and talked with him at length about his thoughts and ideas. We offered him representation then and there – a rarity as it's usually necessary to have some considered discussion between ourselves first. This time, however, there was no doubt.

Needless to say, we were grateful for David's perseverance (and ours) as we drove off into the sunset! back to Toronto. •

DAVID TUCK,
Wynick/Tuck Gallery, Toronto, Ontario, Canada, 1994.

■ Installation: Bess Cutler Gallery, New York

■ Studio assistants: Edward and Pablo

■ Jeff, Alex, Zac, Nicky, Heather and Charlie Bierk, 1987

Peterborough, the ten-year survey show, and knew my work from slides. Finally, they made a studio visit and swiftly and enthusiastically decided to take me on. From that minute on they were incredibly supportive and remain today one of my primary dealers.

DT : But you didn't stop there, David?

DB : No.

DT : The idea of the New York dealer kicked in?

DB : Yes. I returned to New York with my daughter, Heather, who was embarking on a modelling career and wanted to link up with a New York agency. We were both out to conquer the city in much the same way. On our second-to-last day there I came across a beautiful space full of great art on West Broadway. It was the Bess Cutler Gallery and by sheer chance I got my slides into the owner's hands. When I left I was almost certain that she would become my New York dealer (which she did)! That same afternoon Heather, to her great delight, signed a contract with a modelling agency and simultaneously it happened that my son Sebastian and his band won a number of American Music Awards … Only in New York!

DT : [*Laughing*] No kidding, David!

DB : The idea of a network of galleries gradually became very apparent to me. I attribute that to Artspace, and the whole network of ANNPAC galleries [the umbrella organization for the artist-run centres] – we learned to communicate, we learned to interact, we learned to share resources and exhibitions and people. It became so obvious to me. I had this physical space in my studio, I had a limitless number of ideas of things to paint. I am a bit of a workaholic, so I could paint long hours and produce a lot of work. The idea not to depend upon one or two galleries for a living, but to expand that to a controllable number of galleries throughout North America is what I then set out to achieve. It wasn't the kind of strategy that was etched in stone, or thought of and implemented – it evolved naturally. Besides Los Angeles, Toronto, Vancouver, and New York it grew to include the Robert Thomson Gallery in Minneapolis and the Struve Gallery in Chicago, among others.

DT : Okay, just stepping back a bit, the idea of the network – I hadn't realized that before. I can see a connection with the experience of Artspace. It made a lot of sense. One of the things that you must have realized was that you had to put together a team because there was too much work for you to do alone.

DB : When our year's budget at Artspace rose to over one hundred thousand dollars I could not do the books myself, so we hired an accountant. If I was going to start producing paintings for not one but three shows in a year, then I needed a carpenter who could build stretchers, frames and crates so that I could be be free to paint. After two or three years I recognized my strengths and my weaknesses. So, here at my studio, the talented people I have as studio technicians – John Moffat, Patrick Moore, Edward Czmielewski and especially Pablo Ridley – work as a team with the objective of keeping me painting eight to ten hours a day but still in touch with all of the processes supporting my artistic production.

DT : Ten hours a day. What about your family?

DB : My family is the most important thing in my life – my wife especially, and of course my children. When I am asked what my greatest accomplishments are, my part in raising my seven children is at the top of the list. They are what makes all of this worthwhile. To all of them I have tried to pass on my firm belief that if you work hard and apply yourself, doors will open. But I also encourage them to dream and to live out their dreams. I am tremendously proud of each and every one of my children and I think they all possess the ability to do something productive with their lives.

DT : I'm sure you're right. Getting back to your work, I think it is remarkable that it has travelled so much in the past few years – in fact you've been in exhibitions and publications throughout North America and in Europe. The small network that you imagined – Toronto, New York, Los Angeles, Vancouver – has expanded so much. This has led to some interesting commissions.

DB : I've been fortunate to be involved in a number of projects, in part because of the subject matter of my work and its scale. There's been an album cover for Atlantic Records, a giant 24' x 16' portrait of Queen Elizabeth for the I.O.D.E. which hangs in the Peterborough Memorial Centre, and some major commissions for specific sites in Toronto, Phoenix, Versailles, Los Angeles and Tokyo. The best-known of these, at least the most ambitious, hangs in the lobby of the Sheraton Grande Hotel in L.A., a 24' x 22' oil painting which appeared briefly in a recent television mystery movie. I love doing these types of projects because of the challenge they present and because the works themselves live in the public eye. It's the public dialogue that my work invites that makes it suitable for these kinds of projects.

DT : And where is the network right now?

DB : It's at a very interesting state because it is forever shifting and changing. For instance, the Bess Cutler part of it, which was so strong and successful in the beginning, has changed and other players have entered the field. I exhibited with Bess Cutler for two years and she promoted my work through shows in New York, at the Chicago Art Fair and the L.A. Art Fair. Now she acts strictly as a consultant. Galleries that were booming have folded and others have emerged and taken me on. It's a challenge to stay ahead of the game.

DT: I understand you have become famous in Peterborough for your use of the barter system?

DB : It's a system I love and which has allowed me to survive through meagre times. My art has been included in deals from the sale of our house to the purchase of a car. I have a wonderful arrangement here where I trade art for food at our favourite restaurant. It's great! The barter I am most proud of is the art-for-tuition swap with a prep school for my son, Zachary. What pleases me in particular about this deal – beyond the benefits for Zac, of course – is that twice before the school in question turned down offers for barters based on potatoes and printing services!

DT : Going back to the network, you were describing its present state.

DB : I've been very lucky, I've met some wonderful, wonderful people who have believed very strongly in my work and who have done very well with it. The Wynick/Tuck Gallery is at the top of that list. I've also learned that it can be a bit of a roller coaster ride. I've had a San Francisco dealer go bankrupt, I've had a second dealer in the Bay Area decide to close as of this year and so on …

DT : Is there a rebuilding process?

DB : Well, it's in a state of flux. There is a new dealer in San Francisco who is interested in my work, another one in Kansas City who wants to do a show in November, and there has been interest by galleries in Florida and Texas. One thing, one very important thing I pride myself on is the business that we've had to build. If you deal with five or six dealers – very demanding dealers – throughout North America, you have to be very responsible, not only for the work you create but

■ Zachary Bierk

how you look after it in a business sense. I have learned how to say 'no' because not every situation is right and you don't want to overextend yourself.

DT : What do you mean – do less work?

DB : Well, for example, in my first two Toronto exhibitions I wanted to show everything I had, I wanted to put paintings on every inch of the walls, I wanted to come out with both guns blazing, you know? Now, my ideal show would be four walls and four masterpieces. I could continue to do the kinds of paintings I'm doing now and I'm sure I could sell enough of them to keep going and never really have to challenge myself as far as new ideas or experimental approaches are concerned. That doesn't interest me, never has, never will. When you walked into the studio today you saw landscapes that looked as if they might have been created on Mars, totally experimental work. A week ago that didn't exist. I think that's what I'm talking about.

DT : I think what one sees is this beautiful landscape, yet one sees it obliterated by these marks, by these … I don't know how to describe it. There is evidence of some other thing happening. It could have been created on Mars … but there's something more to it …

DB : And it has something to do with my environmental concerns and the whole idea of deconstruction and the veil of history that I'm dealing with. My point is that it would be very easy to fall into a trap of 'success'. I want my art always to be challenging, not only to me but to the dealers I'm working with and the public. That's very important to me. And if you look back to the work I produced when I arrived in Canada, to the first paintings – through to the rocks, to the folds, to the landscapes, and then back to the juxtapositions – you can see almost four-year periods of doing something, probably doing it fairly well and controlling it …

DT : You take it to a certain limit where it seems as if it's as far as you can go – then all of a sudden a crack in the door opens and bang!, you're through into another area. I think the clearest example of this is your painted photographs. I remember you drove to Ottawa and discovered some bare geological formations – rocks – and you painted them, took photographs of

them, and then you actually painted the photographs. And now these new landscapes …

DB : I took four of those paintings down to a show in New York which exhibited the work of eight artists dealing with landscape in the most radical new way – a new way of painting, a new way of seeing, new environmental concerns. And these paintings of mine stood up very well as a whole new body of work. I have this incredible desire to travel across Canada again, taking what I have learned from the landscape through the painted landscape works, through the invented romantic landscapes that I have created, and really revisiting this wonderful and diverse and very beautiful and yet very fragile country.

DT : I like your idea of returning to the source, returning to the landscape, the idea of going across Canada and developing images and ideas from that experience.

DB : As far as the history of Canada is concerned, who better than artists to reflect upon Canada and how wonderful this country is? For me, that exercise would be about the painting of nature and the nature of painting. In other words, you can look at a painting that is an appropriation of a Degas and determine the contemporary context it is placed within, or you can see a totally different picture.

DT : To follow your illustration, one of the things you refer to is the conceptual nature of the work and the situation wherein one person would see a Degas while another would see something else – it's easy to become confused. I think it is more difficult to know exactly what one is seeing. Your painting works on many different levels. What is the context in which the painting is actually situated?

DB : Anyone who looks at my paintings and doesn't read them conceptually as well as literally is missing the entire point. If they look at the technical virtuosity of the painting and do not become engaged in the dialogue then they are missing the point of why I am making these paintings.

DT : I've always said my paintings mean exactly what they say; it's as simple as that and as complicated as that.

DB : But you can't look at your painting and see a canvas with blue paint and white paint. You paint words with images which refer to specific events and to language. You have to read the words and then you have to take it beyond that visual or esthetic level of appreciation and realize the emotional and intellectual reasons behind it.

DT : Do you think your work is understood differently in the U.S. than in Canada?

DB : To a degree. Because my quoted images are usually painted rather than in photographic form, as is more common here in Canada, the perception of my work by some people in this country has been that it is a decorative process of copying original art from old masters. On many more occasions in the U.S. it has been perceived as a totally conceptual process. There are a number of artists, especially American and European, who deal with appropriation – the notions of questioning originality, of recontextualizing and re-presenting imagery – in an attempt to keep a dialogue open with the past and make it more relevant to the present and future. They deal with it in paint as well as in photographic form. Some recent group shows I've been in, such as 'The Purloined Image' at the Flint Institute of the Arts in Michigan and 'Quotations' at the Aldrich Museum in Connecticut, have looked very specifically at this type of work.

DT : Appropriation is a pretty recent phenomenon, David. How exactly did you come to it?

DB : I like to think of myelf as the inventor of appropriation [laughing]. When I started working with 'appropriated' imagery

■ *American Youth Series, Sports Illustrated*, latex and oil on canvas, 8' x 4', 1971

there was no popular critical term for what I was doing, although there was a relationship to Pop Art. I incorporated a magazine cover, a cover from *Sports Illustrated*, into one of my very first major paintings as a graduate student at Humboldt University in 1969. At the same time, I did a seven-foot-diameter circular self-portrait with a background landscape painted from the *Mona Lisa*. From then on it became an element that I used consistently in the body of work that followed – *Venus de Silo*, *Hockey Night in Canada*, the *Laundromat* painting; today it's an integral part of the subject matter of my painting.

DT : It's a new way of seeing, a way of understanding what one is seeing from both inside and outside the frame of the canvas – quite an accomplishment. I jotted down 'veil of history', an interesting phrase you mentioned.

DB : The first time I painted the head of the Vermeer girl – going back to the first show at the Jan Turner Gallery – I painted it the way I paint all of my paintings. I have the photograph in front of me from a postcard or a catalogue or whatever, but always a reproduction. I make a grid, enlarge the scale on the canvas and paint it square by square, repeating the process several times …

DT : Do you draw it first?

DB : No, I just paint it. I maybe draw something within each square but not the whole thing. When this particular image of the Vermeer girl was done I stood back and I looked at it and anatomically it was correct, the colour was correct, the proportion and scale

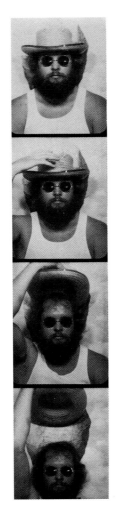

were correct, but it didn't work. I couldn't figure it out. I painted it and I repainted it.

DT : What was wrong?

DB : I had increased the scale from eight inches to four feet but it hadn't aged. If anything, that veil of lines or simulated cracks is going to become very significant, on a larger scale. I sanded the image, imposed trompe l'oeil cracks of paint over it and then it did work. I'm not saying that I have to crack every painting or sand every painting or make every painting look old but I'm aware of it, I'm aware of the physicality of how that looks and how, if you are painting an image from Vermeer, Michelangelo, Degas, you had better do it with integrity and be aware, not try to pull any punches with your audiences. I'm not a forger – if the Fantin-Latour signature is in the source image, it's in my paintings with 'D.B.' right next to it. If there's a crack in it, if there's a decomposed area in it, if there are errors in it then I'm aware of it, too. The originating artist is always given credit in my titles.

DT : But at what point does it become a David Bierk painting?

DB : Well it's created by my hand and from my mind, so to me they always are my paintings. It's a fair question, one that is always asked and often misinterpreted.

DT : There's another way of stating it: the minute you begin to paint something it becomes your painting. What I'm asking, though, concerns the current context within which you are creating these images. When does that become clear?

DB : I hope, the minute people see it, whether in 1994, in 1996 or in the year 2000. People know it's not the original work of art. I am not slavishly redoing the original: it is my own style and paint handling. It's my method of recouping the image for art. The image is what is important. People realize that when, for instance, I alter the scale, put another image next to it, or put a series of works together on the same wall, I'm more concerned with the discourse taking place between the images and all the other things I bring to it – the idea of commodification implied by the magazine covers, the notion of materialism through the use of gold leaf frames, and technology by way of photography, steel and glass. They know it's me choosing the image, choosing the context and then making something new out of it. I hope the experience of my paintings becomes a sanctuary for thought – sometimes it is more successful than others. Because I work very spontaneously, if I have an idea I don't sit around and think about it, I just do it, and I might do it five times until it does work. When it really works it can really move people.

DT : I think what you've done is take away the middle ground. When one looks at your work one really is going to like it or not like it, understand it or not understand it …

DB : People either love it or hate it. To me that is far better than a neutral response.

DT : So, David, it's almost twenty years. What's next? I know you mentioned the trip across Canada.

DB : It will happen, although I can't really say what's next and I think that's very healthy. All I can say is, knock on wood, that I will continue to paint. I have a marvellous family who support me in everything that I do. I feel very very confident and comfortable and strong with the work that I am producing and the system within which I am working. As long as the painting I hang on the wall today is better than the one I hung yesterday, then I feel I'm working in the right direction. I have a lot of energy, I have the support of my family, I have this structure around me that I hope will keep me working like a mad fool for another ten, twenty, thirty, maybe fifty years, who knows?

THE ALLEGORIST

followed by

MAJOR PAINTINGS 1987-1994

with additional texts by David Bierk

Time is a concept by which we measure our pain
(Art & Money),
to Manet, Picasso and Lorrain
oil on canvas
44½" x 106"
1989
Collection: McCarthy Tetrault, Toronto, Ont.

by Daniel Sharp

THE ALLEGORIST

A RT historical images and images from mass media have been themes in David Bierk's work throughout his career. Bierk appropriates images from the canon of codified art master-works, gleaning them – and related pictures of culture – from various modes of reproduction: from books, magazines, posters, postcards and other kinds of photo-graphically accessible formats. In Bierk's hands, these images, culled from bewilderingly diverse and sundry sources, are repainted, combined, juxtaposed, and otherwise employed in new contexts. In the particular and characteristic way he uses his chosen images, Bierk's role is that of the *allegorist*.

Allegory is essentially *extended metaphor*, a figurative narra-tive or description (or implication) conveying, in the case of painting, through layering and echoing, a suggestive moral meaning. In allegory, one resonating meaning is amplified or modified or intensified by means of the application of another resonating meaning adjacent to the first. In Bierk's employment of the allegorical mode, paintings from the history of art and images from mass media are combined in a manner which, however fragmentary, intermittent or chaotic, nevertheless comes together somehow (often, one feels, by force of will of the painter himself) to produce – in accumulation – meaningful statements, different from the intentions of the artists who are his sources, but relevant today. As critic Craig Owens has suggested, the two fundamental assumptions upon which the allegorical method proceeds are a conviction about the remote-ness of the past and, simultaneously, a desire to redeem that past for use in the present. That such a set of assumptions is the basis of David Bierk's program as a painter will, I hope, become clear in the course of the discussion that follows.

The images Bierk employs in his work have already – before his use of them – been transformed from what they were origi-

■ *Grid Studies: From Tintoretto, Van der Weyden, Cézanne, Titian, Correggio, Masaccio*, oil on photos on board, 20½" x 16½" each, 1993
Collection: Serge Darkanzali, Calgary, Alta.

nally by the circumstances of reproduction in general, and in particular by the process of being photographed. The images Bierk decides to use in his work are already, as he comes upon them, serving a secondary purpose. As reproductions, they serve a scholarly purpose, or a commercial purpose, or they may serve as pivot-points of ideological persuasiveness. These reproductions are, in other words, already using high-art images in powerful and purposeful ways. None of them could ever be mistaken for an unmediated or entirely transparent representation of the original work of art. Bierk's use of the reproduced image is already a second or third generation appropriation. As such, his use of art historical imagery can be seen as a redemptive intervention in the past. It is a *re-use* of art history as a framework for the recovery of the work from its first dislocations. While the meaning is changed from the original, Bierk reclaims the imagery from the distracted condition of a reproduction to the charged field of fine art, specifically as a new painted object.

The address to history in Bierk's paintings takes place in a contemporary context, one in which post-modern theoretical positions make continual proclamation of 'the end of history'. A complex and multi-valent concept, the notion of the end of history turns on the assumption that history is a constructed narrative made up of certain systems of choice, certain systematic exclusions and reductions. The whole project of History is such a value-laden enterprise that it is increasingly difficult to lend uncritical support to what we used to think of as historical truth. And of course the History of Art is one of the grand narratives now undergoing a critical examination whereby the hitherto silent ideological circumstances that produced the narrative itself are detached and probed in a search for the nature of their fictive authority. This is, in essence, deconstruction. And although contemporary art criticism's assault on the bulwarks of Art History remains a fascinating project, the status of painting as a contemporary cultural practice is increasingly thrown into a system of nested ambiguities leading to a crisis of popular esteem, of credibility.

Given such a cultural climate and, adding to that, the relative inaccessibility of the 'real' masterpieces of the western tradition, it is easy enough to see how reproductions in art books and magazines have come to make up a great part of the cultural environment of David Bierk and other Canadian artists, especially those who live outside the larger centres of art. Bierk's painted appropriations of magazine covers featuring works of art are – like his apparently more 'innocent' landscape paintings – representations of value, signs of Art, an exploration of the reign of the inaccessible. Such appropriations are both genuine thefts of the images of art and, simultaneously, the resurrection of these images as 'real paintings' again. Bierk is responding forcefully, even passionately, to the redirecting of the original meaning of a work of art when it appears on the cover of a magazine, where it is cropped, reduced in size and overlaid with type. His strategy is to invert this misuse of the original work by re-appropriating the art image along with the magazine on which it appeared, even including the computer-readable pricing code in the corner. Thus is the original appropriation re-appropriated. This perversity results in the exposure of the role of the art object as ideological carrier, and makes explicit the ways in which high art is employed as a means of generating (for a magazine, for example) prestige, influence and, finally, saleability. The use of art in advertising practices and the smooth and seductive packaging of art – or Great Art – by museums and national galleries is handily addressed and analyzed by Bierk's paintings by means – and this is the true source of both the perversity and the charm of his works – of the degree to which the paintings are themselves made complicit in this production of value. Bierk's painting practice reveals a fascination with the vast spectacular systems of art history, taste, style, fashion, luxury and wealth. And it is by means of the allegorical process of juxtaposing fragments of appropriated imagery that Bierk is able to reveal the connections and interactions within the larger sign systems of culture.

THE ARCHEOLOGIST

To paint images of the past is a way to recover them for the present. The historical work of art is thus recuperated in a changed form. In Bierk's hands, the historical image does not merely have its original meaning restored to it; rather, additional meaning is added to that image, meaning that is relevant to Bierk himself and the context within which he produces his work. A new entity is created. While Bierk contends that his use of art-historical imagery is part of a dialogue with the past, the process of allegory overwrites the original artwork with new contexts and thus new meanings. Bierk's use of appropriated imagery is powered by a desire and indeed a genuine longing to reify Art, to make Art live again. While the photographic image of a work of art is not in itself valuable (though it *is* likely meaningful), it is the image (the sign) of value. To remake a painting while working from a photographic image of that original painting is to approach closer to the possession of value. This poignant homage to the unattainable masterwork and its reacquisition through the strategies of appropriation gains power and meaning as an act of self-consciousness by a painter in the late twentieth century living in a small Canadian city. Identified as such, it is all the more possible to see Bierk working out personal issues of claiming, caring, acquisition and exposure in his paintings. It is thus all the more possible to understand the stylistic forms and procedural strategies he employs.

As Director of Artspace, David Bierk spent thirteen years producing and organizing over a hundred exhibitions and art-related projects in the community. It was not until 1986 that Bierk turned away from the needs and pressures of Artspace in order to direct his considerable energies into his own painting. His intentions, however, remained much the same: to make art and art history real in the place where he lived. Having made the decision to concentrate on producing paintings which incorporated images from other art, Bierk brought to bear upon his own works all of his previous passion for framing, exhibiting, juxtaposing, and recontextualizing works of art. The impulse to curate, to select, to exhibit art was thus shifted to the gleaning of images from art history for his own uses. The urgency of using art history is made all the more intense for Bierk by the relative absence of high art in the daily life of the community where he lives – which is no more and no less than a shard of the normal Canadian socio-cultural landscape.

Bierk's desire for a different reality and for additional or other cultural values (which represents a kind of idealism that is perhaps common among artists) is projected onto a plane of art discourse that leads him strategically to appropriate the free-floating signs of culture which he finds reproduced all around him. In effect, Bierk sets himself up in opposition to the cultural landscape in which he finds himself in Canada, and is led to create a fantasy of the masterpieces of art history. What is revealed by this expression of parallel desire within David Bierk's painting is an *absence*.

IN THE ABSENCE OF PARADISE

Working spontaneously, freely, and intuitively, Bierk deploys images of artworks for which he has long held affection, as well as additional images he comes across which serve in some way to provoke him. The process is energetic, eclectic, and brash, and produces an impression of reckless plunder, a sort of aesthetic piracy. In his work, Bierk intends to raise questions about contemporary social issues, issues pertaining to the family, the environment (both physical and social), and the nature of cultural practice at large. On another level, however, Bierk works out of a kind of headlong joy in and love for the history of painting itself. It is in some way the shimmering *history* of painting in which Bierk desires to be a full participant, and we might reasonably suggest that it is this *idea* of painting that he loves more than the historical *paintings* themselves. The space of history in which Bierk desires to participate is coloured with pure and simple intentions, with life-affirming purpose, with freedom and innocence; it is a virtual paradise of potential. And a paradise lost, or to a large extent absent. It is to the absence of this paradisiacal state, this state of grace, that Bierk's paintings are addressed, and it is this absence and the related *desire* that attends it which inform the yearning, the longing, with which the artist's work is so powerfully suffused.

PAINTING AS TEXT

Inasmuch as some of the appeal of David Bierk's paintings lies in their use of imagery from art history, the prestige and the cachet of the famous and rare are borrowed for new purposes. For any frequenter of the world's great art museums, for whom a viewing of, say, a Vermeer is within the realm of expectations, Bierk's robust and unabashed appropriations of Vermeer (clearly a Bierk favourite) might well appear to be thefts and travesties. But the apprehension of a true Vermeer painting is an altogether rare experience, those few paintings being geographically distant and culturally remote. So for most viewers of David Bierk's paintings, for whom Vermeer's paintings may be a sign of great value, rarity, and the unique product of a master vision, and who may also be enamoured of the content of the paintings – a quiet bourgeois domesticity viewed in exquisite clarity – Bierk's paintings employing a Vermeer image once again present a *real object* rather than an absent masterpiece, an attainable image of something of *real value*, a new Vermeer (or Manet or Degas, etc.).

The Bierk-masterpiece is an object/painting which substitutes uneasily for the original, becoming within that calculus of unease something else, something more real, more vivid: a masterwork with added contemporary cultural overlay. Bierk's appropriations of art historical images rescue masterworks from cultural *distance*, perhaps from cultural irrelevance, bringing

them back by hand to live again in a new political and social context. Inevitably, Bierk's aggressive utilization and deployment of art history does not work for everybody. It works for Bierk himself as a producer because of his specific context, but it seems to me that Bierk's paintings signify something quite different depending upon where they are shown and who is looking at them. While the strategy of appropriation creates new meanings by the recontextualization of historical works of art, it would seem that the articulation of a new context can be only partly a function of the paintings themselves. It is here that the viewer's role as a spectator in a specific time and place becomes crucial. Because of the degree of free and unrestrained contextual play, it is understandable that the allegorical narratives of Bierk's paintings depend on where the work is seen, and to a most important extent, on the participating interpretive energies and sympathies of the viewers.

■ *Study: Woman Holding a Balance, To Vermeer,* fibreglas resin over oil on book and steel, 12" x 9", 1993

MAJOR PAINTINGS 1987-1994

Alexander Contemplating Why U.F.O.s Don't Land Here Anymore: to Caspar David Friedrich, Albert Bierstadt, John William Casilear, Frederic Edwin Church and T.E. Pfliger is a work in which Blind History is represented by the grandly over-sized depiction of an antique stone statue of Alexander the Great. The eyes are blank and unseeing. Arranged on one side of the painting are re-workings of four landscapes by the artists Friedrich, Bierstadt, Casilear, and Church. These re-paintings, stacked one above the other, speak as a group of past glory, the grandeur of romance, the historic sublimity of ruin and the passing of heroism and heroic vision. One of the notions implied in the use of the particular paintings assembled here is that history is a fading, no longer apprehendable matrix. The extravagant title of the painting hints at the notion that the present age has lost a good deal of its capacity for fantasy and much of its imaginative capability. The surplus of connotations brimming from the painting spills out in several different directions. The picture is typical of many of Bierk's allegorical essays in its refusal to tell a complete and specific story. There is no single answer to the questions raised by the painting, no single correct solution by which the painting might be cracked open under the pressure of analysis and made to lay itself bare. But the fecund piling up of fragments and the collision of a number of different stories within the picture open up the possibility of a discourse that makes interpretation of the painting *seem possible*. This flickering *potential* in Bierk's work is one of the factors that lends a complex attractiveness to the painter's employment of the allegorical method. – D.S.

Alexander Contemplating
Why U.F.O.s Don't
Land Here Anymore:
to Caspar David Friedrich,
Albert Bierstadt,
John William Casilear,
Frederic Edwin Church
and T.E. Pfliger
oil on canvas
108" x 108"
1987
Collection: Marshall and Patricia Geller,
Los Angeles, Calif.

Both *Paradise Lost I, to Michelangelo, Bierstadt, Eakins, Inness and Heade* and *Paradise Lost II, to Michelangelo, Kensett, Cole, Sarasov and Gauguin* are related to *Alexander Contemplating ...* (preceding page) and are, in the main, large paintings of two Michelangelo heads. The original sculpture and drawing have now been painted by Bierk on a hugely increased scale. One painting imitates the sculpted surface of the stone, while the other imitates the marks of the drawing itself in paint and brushwork. Like the head of Alexander the Great and that of the Egyptian boy (p. 65), these heads are hyper-realized in a complex quadripartite homage to the original artists, to the greatness of the original works of art, and to the glory (as we see it now through the somewhat tarnished and diminishing spectacles of the late twentieth century) of those long past times. The historical landscapes stacked up the sides of the paintings speak eloquently – and, as in so many of Bierk's paintings, plangently – about the passing away of the very landscapes they depict. The dying of the light and the waning of the day are metaphors for, among other things, the retreat of the virtues and values of some mythical, glorious age gone by. In works like these, the heroism of the past is glorified, even while – and it is this that keeps Bierk's paintings from growing sentimental – the choice of subsidiary paintings within the compositions (particularly those of Albert Bierstadt and Heade here) acknowledge that the wish for heaven (or for paradise at least) may be an enterprise unlikely to succeed. All in all, the faithless present, the site of a culture-wide ennui, makes those unruly desires and fantasies inherent in Bierk's choices of historical paintings to reposition and re-present, the locus of a profound melancholy and a bitter-sweet sense of nostalgia. – D.S.

Paradise Lost II,
to Michelangelo,
Kensett, Cole,
Sarasov and Gauguin
oil on canvas
96" x 108"
1988
Collection: Ann and Leland Verner,
Toronto, Ont.

Paradise Lost I,
to Michelangelo,
Bierstadt, Eakins,
Inness and Heade
oil on canvas
96" x 108"
1988
Collection: Axl Rose,
Los Angeles, Calif.

During the winter of 1880, painter Edouard Manet, then in his forty-ninth year, began to die of a body-wasting disease. His strength was diminished in his last years and he worked more slowly and on a smaller scale. In the last months of his life, between 1881 and his death in 1883, Manet painted sixteen exquisite small-scale still-lifes, most of them painted after floral bouquets which were gifts from friends.

In 1986 David Bierk's wife, Liz, received as a gift from her father the book *The Last Flowers of Manet*, by Robert Gordon and Andrew Forge (Abrams, 1986), a handsome volume devoted to a discussion and the fine reproduction of this series of paintings. The book reproduced all the late flower paintings for the first time, gathered from public and private collections around the world. David Bierk was inspired by the book, moved by the fact that although Manet was ill and dying, his pictures are charged with vitality, brimming with life and energy.

Bierk set about to paint the last flowers of Manet, copying from carefully gridded reproductions from the book. Eventually he painted – or re-painted – all sixteen works. The paintings were shown together as a series for the first time at the Jan Turner Gallery in Los Angeles in 1988. Since then Bierk has painted a number of them again, showing and selling them singly, using them in juxtaposition with other paintings in larger compositions, and re-assembling the entire series again in exhibition at the Ottawa Art Gallery, Ottawa in 1992.

Bierk feels affinity and sympathy for Manet at numerous junctures. Many of Manet's paintings involved a transformation or paraphrase from earlier works Manet found stimulating as source material. Manet had been accused of plagiarizing the Spanish masters, and in a painting such as *Déjeuner sur l'herbe (Luncheon on the Grass)*, for example, he had borrowed elements of the composition from Raphael via Marcantonio and from Giorgione. So in Bierk's view, Manet's references to earlier models is one of the precedents for Bierk's own contemporary appropriations.

Bierk also admires the direct and 'modern' way in which Manet's paint handling speaks. Instead of rendering a flower, the paint and brushwork *form* a flower. Manet was a painter of his time, linking a history of painting with the modern painting impulse to translate one's sensations immediately. The serial character which Manet's last still-lifes seem to have (especially when presented in a book) is to Bierk both a marvelous process and an inspiration.

Finally, Bierk re-employs the late still-life flowers of Manet as symbols in the usual way that flowers are emblems of beauty, purity, fecundity, and the shortness of life. The Manet flowers are charged with life and energetically painted even as Manet's strength and life were waning. They are poignant and perfect eulogies, which Bierk intends in his reuse of them as a broad comment on the waning strengths and shifting powers of contemporary life. – D.S.

Fleurs dans un vase,
from the *Last Flowers of Manet* series
oil on canvas
22" x 14⅛"
1987
Collection: James Lodge and Assoc.,
Irvine, Calif.

Left:

From the Last Flowers of Manet
oil on canvas
24" x 96"
1987
Collection: Ann and Leland Verner,
Toronto, Ont.

These paintings are typical of a body of work I produced in the late 1980s in which I combined still-lifes and images by Gauguin with glass and plywood.

I first saw Fantin-Latour's work at an exhibition at the National Gallery of Canada some years ago and was drawn to the eloquent and peaceful beauty of his flower paintings and his 'modern' way of applying the paint. Unlike the finicky detail of the Dutch and Flemish schools, this style of painting gave the illusion of reality using the physicality of the paint itself. The Fantin-Latour flowers, like their Manet counterparts, reinforce the idea of a eulogy for a lost time, or place, or art, or culture.

The Gauguin images also evoke this lost paradise, the small proportions behind glass emphasizing preciousness and fragility. The surrounding plywood, roughly plastered and then stained in an enclosure, evokes the infringement on primitive life by industrialized man in the name of progress. – D.B.

In the Absence of Paradise,
to Gauguin and Fantin-Latour I
oil on canvas, oil on plaster
on plywood
84" x 114"
1989
Collection: Paul and Veva Guerin,
Los Angeles, Calif.

Flash Art Triptych

oil on canvas and metal leaf

41" x 79"

1987

The painting *Flash Art Triptych* deals with the functions and uses of art and is straightforward about the contradictions it reveals. The triptych format alludes to the art-historical tradition of religious altar-painting. A painting of a *Flash Art* magazine cover is here flanked by paintings of two *House & Garden* covers. Reproduced on the *Flash Art* cover was part of an Andy Warhol painting of Leonardo da Vinci's *The Last Supper*. Bierk has thus copied in paint a magazine's appropriation of one painter's appropriation of another painting. At one stroke, Bierk is able to invoke and pay an ironic homage to a whole series of nested flames: *Flash Art* – as a name for trendy commercialized fine art, Andy Warhol, Leonardo, and the famous participants of *The Last Supper*. Flanking this holy party (which has become a kind of sacred sediment at the bottom of the overlays) are the trappings of the lesser but still powerful functions of late twentieth-century art – as embellishment for houses and gardens.

At the left of the triptych is reproduced a *House & Garden* cover showing a photo of a modern living-room scene with plants and a coffee table and attendant objects. In this room setting hangs a David Hockney painting, which is a picture of a coffee table with objects on it, looking like nothing so much as a celebration of living-room decor. Here is the triumph of decor – now curtailed or amplified, depending upon where you stand in these matters, by the fact that the right panel of the triptych holds a *House & Garden* cover on which is reproduced a painting of a field of poppies by Claude Monet. Is this levelling or elevation? And if so, of what and by means of what? Here is interior set off by exterior, house balanced by garden. It is also, however, a presentation of art master-work balanced (the word now contains new poignancy) by up-market bric-a-brac. The furnish-

Art in America Triptych
oil on canvas, oil on board
26" x 44" overall
1987
Collection: Lynne Wynick and
David Tuck, Toronto, Ont.

ings of the interior, including the Hockney painting, and the representation of country-side leisure activity in the Monet painting, and the Monet painting itself are all signs of value, wealth, and social status. At this point the Bierk painting can be said to take on a certain elegiac weight or satirical thrust, depending upon the nature of the viewer's sensibilities. As a means of emphasizing the already clear message of the triumph of wealth and commodity value over historical meaning, while maintaining at the same time a whiff of the fragrance of the sacred, now irretrievably intermingled with the commercial sublime, Bierk has floated the *Flash Art* cover over a rectangle of gold leaf.

The sustaining contradiction in Bierk's work into which he jumps unabashedly is that he himself cherishes the history of art, and venerates da Vinci, Warhol, Monet and Hockney; he avidly looks at the reproductions of paintings in *Flash Art* and other magazines to see what is being done in contemporary art and to see what is being promoted; and it is with full self-consciousness of the irony in laying out these paintings in a sacred format, associating them with gold, appropriating them for himself, that his practice is complicit with the acts of appropriation of the magazine's designers and producers. Bierk's work is saved from plagiarism and rescued from simple seduction and nostalgic charm by the way his paintings reveal the mechanisms at work in this use of artworks by the magazines' producers. In the not untroubling presentation of these images of art, we are forced to reconsider how contemporary painting functions and how it is used in our society. – D.S.

Art in America

May 1990 $4.75

**J.-L. DAVID:
3 VIEWS**

**ART &
OBSCENITY**

**TUCKER, JAFFE,
LEVITT**

À MARÀT.

DAVID.

ART, OBJECT, COMMODITY, 1988, employs a sequence of appropriated images in order to provide a critique of the commodification of cultural products. A chance perusal of an art journal led Bierk to this splendid image of the head of an Egyptian boy. The original funerary memento, now in Berlin, is fashioned on a wooden panel with paint and gold leaf. Working from a photographic reproduction of the work, Bierk made a nearly exact replica on his own wooden panel and subsequently placed it in a small museum-like display unit. This is thus a representation of the original work.

This same icon-like image was then painted again, this time on a gigantic, epic scale, transforming the portrait from a modest devotional or commemorative relic to an aggrandized art object. With the exaggeration of scale and a certain congruent augmentation of the power of the original object, Bierk intensifies certain characteristics of the original painting in order to direct attention to its elemental beauty and its exotic charm, part of which is, of course, the excellence of the ancient and anonymous icon-maker's craftsmanship. The original work has now been literally blown out of all proportion, suggesting that it is the museum itself, the intensification process that curating bestows upon a collected or retrieved object, that is being celebrated, or at least examined. The big head is a billboard advertising the fact of ancient artistic grace, beauty, and the love of life.

The third element in the composition is a metal printing-plate prepared with an image of the cover of the Toronto-based art journal *C Magazine*. Onto this pearlescent gray plate is painted the shape of the gold background and the garland from the Egyptian head. What is being said here? Possibly that in our time, the primary has been replaced by the secondary, the analytical. Written below the image of the magazine cover is the word 'COMMODITY'. Bierk is suggesting that it is the character of the art magazine to commodify art. In this work, Bierk speaks in his most literal of allegorical voices. – D.S.

COMMODITY

Seine River Series,

to Monet

oil on canvas

72" x 78"

1990

Collection: N.Y.N.E.X., New York, N.Y.

The first time I was profoundly moved by a Monet painting was at the Museum of Modern Art in New York when I walked into the 'waterlilies room'. It became immediately apparent that the work is all about painting and less about water than about how Monet saw and how he painted.

Some years later, a trip to Giverny further lodged Monet in my subconscious. When I finally came to quote his work it was not only because of the particular beauty or importance of a single image, but rather because the works lent themselves to being collected in groups or sequences. Their beauty and sense of place were, for me, secondary to the formal exercise of examining the method of their creation.

Most recently I have broken up the grid and strip of Monet images with panels of steel, so that the landscape as a way of seeing is virtually destroyed, both literally and metaphorically. The series is no longer an integral whole but has passed some point of no return in terms of its viability as an attainable end. – D.B.

A Distant Light,

Poplars, to Monet

oil on canvas on plywood

36" x 115"

1990

Private collection

A Family Portrait, to the Bwami tribe, Degas, and Freud, 1989.
The main subject of the Degas painting reproduced here is the
complex of relationships – what Freud himself called 'the family
romance' – between the members of the bourgeois Bellelli family.
Bierk has extended and amplified certain relationships between
members of the family, raising their interactions onto an allegorical level where dark, possibly sexual desires, unspoken
promptings, inchoate urges come together to form an essay about
the nature of middle-class propriety and taboo. The Degas
composition is already psychologically charged because of the
relative remoteness of the father, who sits apart from the rest of
the family. As if in answer to the threat of the father's unknowa-
bility, the mother has placed her hand protectively on the
shoulder of one of the daughters. Bierk has interposed a disturbing erasure in the middle of the canvas, causing the face of the
young woman to be blurred, putting into question her identity
and position in the family at large.

The Bwami tribe mask and the image of Sigmund Freud
that flank the central panel are related inasmuch as each of them
is a *sign* of a certain kind of understanding of the primal human
imagination. The tribal mask emerging from a mysterious
passage of darkness is, for Bierk, an emblem of exoticism and
strangeness – an emblem of the Other and an entrance point,
perhaps, into a more fundamental comprehension of the nature
of human desire and its motivations. The painting of a black and
white photograph of Freud, the 'father of psychoanalysis', is
offered as a balance.

Now, on one level the image of the 'primitive' tribal mask
and the image of the modern psychiatrist may represent opposite
poles of understanding of human beings' actions. But we are not
sure if it is the intention of the juxtaposition to comment on the
variety of ways and means there may be to explain and understand human behaviour, or, more likely, to show us that in spite
of the range of attempts that have been made to explain

Left:

A Family Portrait,

to the Bwami tribe,

Degas and Freud

oil on canvas

54" x 138"

1989

Collection: Central Guaranty Trust,

Toronto, Ont.

Below:

Portrait of a Father/Daughter,

to the Bwami tribe,

Degas and Freud

oil on canvas

54" x 133"

1989

Collection: Steve and Julia Shifman,

Cincinnati, Ohio

ourselves, human behaviour and our most intimate thoughts and feelings can still be surprising, disturbing, and difficult to control. There is much that we do not know and cannot explain. Do these two image/signs of the mask and the doctor suggest the failure of any adequate interpretation of human action? How can the feelings and thoughts that compose the complex of relations between members of a family be understood? In what way could Bierk, as the artist, be exploring the theme of the relationship between a father and a daughter, looking through Degas, but speaking of himself? – D.S.

I first saw the Floorscrapers painting by Gustave Caillebotte in 1982 at the De Young Museum in San Francisco as part of a small collection of European art.

I was immediately attracted by the subject matter of the painting which was entirely different from the traditional still-lifes, portraits and landscapes that surrounded it. The image of men scraping floors challenged my sense of beauty, but what fascinated me most was the merging of this content with its form. The way it was painted struck me as very modern in its concept. The floor as the subject matter, rendered in paint, with paint peeling away from the floor, depicted in paint, and the physicality of wood chips, also painted, was a perfect balance of conceptual and literal elements.

I also realized that the act of scraping the surface of the floor paralleled my concerns for man's stripping of the planet and the resulting demise of art and creativity. Robert Hughes refers to this situation as the 'strip-mining of culture'.

My painted quotation of the Floorscrapers encompassed all of these notions. It was produced on the heels of my *Save the Planet Imaginary Landscape* series and just as I was beginning to use historical imagery from art in juxtaposition with landscapes and still-life works. The first version of the Floorscrapers was paired with my painting of a William Keith landscape image in a vertical composition. Keith was a nineteenth-century California landscape painter whose work I first saw in a small university museum in the San Francisco Bay area. The second and third variations used the floorscrapers images surrounded by broad 'frames' of trompe l'oeil wallpaper, and were deliberately installed in front of large windowed walls at the Wynick/Tuck Gallery, playing on the juxtaposition of the real and the painted, the historical and the contemporary. – D.B.

Before I produced the *Ryder Boat Series*, I had been aware of Ryder's work but really only associated his name with a few images which I found mysterious and appealing. I was prompted to do this body of work after I bought a book on Ryder and felt an immediate response to his marine images. In particular I was interested in the work as a series of paintings in much the same way that I had been drawn to the Manet flowers and Monet's poplar, Seine River and Rouen Cathedral series.

My attraction to series works comes from a desire to examine the process of art. While I am interested in the historical relationship of painters to nature, I have been preoccupied with how they invented ways of painting nature. To be able to view a whole body of work by an artist on one subject amplifies the exploration of the process. It reveals an entire approach to the genre, a way of seeing and a way of painting. This point of view is in part a hangover from my thirteen years as the director of Artspace and perhaps has its roots in my art education. I was always in search of curatorial meaning beyond a single work of art, whether in my own graduate show which was entitled 'American Youth Series', or in the compilation of work by other artists.

I found the Ryder paintings spiritually charged and profoundly beautiful. I was also drawn to the artist's dark and moody approach to the landscape. But as I began to paint my Ryder series, and studied the painting surfaces closely (in repro-

duction form), I found that the deterioration of those surfaces became the focus of my attention – their pockmarks and cracks became a symbolic statement on the state of the planet. Then, as with the Monet and Manet works, when sixteen Ryder images were painted and hung in a row a new perceptual involvement was immediately possible. The paintings read like a poem, or music, or a film strip. New associations and new abstract compositional elements emerged from the body of work.

A great irony of my Ryder series was its showing in New York which coincided by pure chance with a major Ryder exhibition at the Brooklyn Museum! Of course I was delighted by these circumstances and intrigued by seeing this work first-hand. – D.B.

The tripartite format of *Bouquet de juliennes et fruits (White Rockets and Fruit), to Africa, Fantin-Latour, and de Chirico* recalls the form of an altar. The central image in this composition is a greatly over-sized still-life painting originally created by Fantin-Latour. In Bierk's rendition the scale is purposely excessive (the peaches are monstrous in size), delicacy is blown up, and Fantin-Latour's gentle bourgeois essay on fecundity and beauty is exploded to billboard size.

It is curious that those of us who live in North America admire so fondly the civilized flowers and fruit of a nineteenth-century European still-life painting by Fantin-Latour – the imagery of fruitful bounty, beauty, order and luxury, and the reminder that one would do well to contemplate the fleetingness of flowers, fruits and life itself. It might occur to us that such an

White Rockets and Fruit, to Africa,

Fantin-Latour, and de Chirico

oil on canvas

74" x 158"

1990

Collection: Pierre Luc St. Laurent and

David Allan Hill, Ottawa, Ont.

image is not a container of contemporary values and truth. The recognition of this in the face of the re-painting of the nineteenth-century work not only imbues the Bierk composition with some nostalgia, but also creates an air of menace for the viewer now forced to contemplate the absence and dissolution of those formerly secure and central social values.

Flanking the central still-life are smaller black and white paintings mounted inside framing panels, paintings which appear to offer, in the bluntest and most forceful manner, attacks – from different directions – on the assumptions and beliefs inherent in the Fantin-Latour work. On the left side is a painting over a photograph of an African tribal woman who is herself painted and tattooed. She functions here as the nineteenth-century embodiment of 'the primitive'. On the right side of the large composition, Bierk has painted a version of a de Chirico painting of a manikin, a twentieth-century meditation on the mechanization of life. The de Chirico figure is a techno-meta-physical expression of a savage modern century – a century that has witnessed and will continue to witness unimaginable human suffering and war. De Chirico's painting is offered as a challenge to the formerly secure values of the average nineteenth-century European.

Bierk's composition is finally a lament for the passing of certitude, of fixed cultural values, and embraces the debate in which 'the natural primitive' and the modernist primitive symbolically represent a challenge to the cultural assumptions and norms of white Euro-centred Art History. – D.S.

La Ville Louvre, to Manet

oil on canvas,

oil on photo

30¾" x 60"

1992

Private collection

In the work titled *La Ville Louvre, to Manet*, 1992, the central image is an enlarged painted photograph of a scene in one of the galleries of the Louvre Museum. The photo shows a worker preparing to haul on a rope in order to raise an enormous painting from a face-down position on the floor to an upright place on the gallery wall. In the background a painting of a crucifixion rests on the floor, leaning against the wall, ready to be hung. The viewer may discover a certain wry irony in the comparison of the painting of Christ hanging on the cross with the portrayal of the gallery room where paintings are about to be hung on the walls.

To the right of this central scene is a Bierk version of one of Manet's last flower paintings, a modest bouquet that provides the eulogistic note in the composition. The 'Manet' flowers are framed within a wide border of unpainted steel which is

balanced on the left side of the composition by another rectangle of steel fastened with evenly spaced bolts. The steel functions as a sign of strength, permanence, impenetrability and closure. Bierk's use of steel as a framing device signifies by its material character the grip of the museum and the security of the canons of art history.

In this allegorical picture, the Louvre, as one of the world's great museums, is the solid repository, the final stop in the production of historical value, and the temple of the history of art. This behind-the-scenes picture is a glimpse of the museum at work, literally and metaphorically hoisting paintings to their proper places of importance. Thus in some way it can be ventured that the museum is the site where painting – Art – is crucified even as it is resurrected. – D.S.

A Eulogy to Art, The Sculpture Class,
to Fantin-Latour
oil on canvas,
oil on photos
28" x 60"
1992
Collecton: Stephanie and Larry Jacobson,
Kansas City, Mo.

In the *Eulogy to Art* series of juxtaposed and constructed paintings, Bierk typically employs a floral still-life as a kind of framing commentary to his selection of an appropriated image from art history or painted photograph. The subject of these juxtapositions is always art and the history of art. Other elements frequently find their way into the works, which end up incorporating textured panels, steel plates and collaged passages of architectural detail. A eulogy is an expression of praise, and is sometimes, though not always, associated with the death of the subject. Here, Bierk continues the themes from his earlier work, praising and paying homage to various artists and, more particularly, to works of art he reveres. In the Eulogy series he continues to refine and develop his commentary on the character and the nature of art and art-making. These works seem also to speak about the contemporary role of the artist in general and of certain matters pertaining to Bierk's own role as a painter.

In *A Eulogy to Art, David Watching, to Fantin-Latour*, Bierk has enlarged a newspaper photograph of seven men carrying a large painting through the streets of Florence. The photograph is taken from high above and behind the famous copy of Michelangelo's *David* that stands on the steps of Florence's Palazzo Vecchio. The men in the photograph may well be rescuing the painting from some danger, such as the flooding which threatened so many of the city's art treasures in recent times.

The viewer, however, is not told anything more specific about the situation. The scene tells us something about the perilous dislocation and ultimate rescue of one particular painting. Allegorically, it may be that all painting, or the idea of Art, is threatened and thus requires rescue; or it may be that Bierk is suggesting that art is continually in peril and needs constant and ongoing saving.

Part of the painting's title, 'David Watching', is rich with implication. The original statue of David is a heroic masterpiece of art history – an eighteen-foot sculpture from the early sixteenth century celebrating youth, strength, and courage. The

story of David, of course, is that of the young man who, against all odds, defeated an enemy giant and released his people from peril. It would not be irrelevant to suggest that David, watching, could also refer to the painter himself, which adds both a certain heroism and a certain close-up poignancy to the allegorical mix. Whatever hope the story contains, there is a certain melancholy within the story as Bierk uses the imagery here, that inevitably attaches itself to the passivity of watching. The offering of a bouquet of flowers (the still-life by Fantin-Latour) elaborates this sentiment of helplessness, appending notions of homage and eulogy. – D.S.

A Eulogy to Art, David Watching,
to Fantin-Latour
oil on canvas, oil on
plaster on plywood,
oil on photo
54" x 138"
1989
Collection: Art Gallery of Peterborough,
Peterborough, Ont.

Upon seeing the original of this famous Degas painting, Bierk was transfixed by its power. Rather unlike any other painting by Degas, the privacy of the moment depicted here is almost illicit in its intensity, that intensity being underscored by a richly enigmatic, ominous mood. Bierk says he found himself fascinated by the tension and mystery of the relationship between the male and female subjects of the work. He was also struck by what he felt was the painting's oddness, given the time in which it was painted, and by its apparent peculiar relevance to the problems of domestic violence and sexual abuse which are the objects of so much current media attention. Though sometimes referred to as 'The Rape' *(Le viol)*, the true subject of the painting and the nature of Degas' intentions for it are the subject of debate by art-historians, and the issue has never been decided.

Because Bierk saw in the painting's concealed or repressed narrative a potential commentary on the contemporary social concern of sexual harassment and violence, he decided to repaint the image in a scale where the figures are nearly life-size, extravagantly larger than the original work. The idea of this almost theatrical presentation was to impose the scene upon the viewer and at the same time to confront the viewer physically. The theatricality and sense of literalness in the picture are emphasized by the addition of an old Gothic-styled church window frame, an actual architectural detail from a church. This is placed beside the Degas scene over a gold ground. There is also, in what is by now a kind of signature-like addendum in Bierk's painting of this period, a still-life painting of a vase of flowers after Fantin-Latour.

The string of juxtaposed images creates a virtual allegory of the domestic. The tension and threat of implied violence are set within the bedroom, close to the church, eulogized with flowers. The flowers speak of fertility and beauty, of meditation and mortality. The church window against its gold ground hints at the power of the sacred in human affairs. These passages together contribute – in aggregate – a sense of comfort and refuge, all of which is powerfully challenged and compromised and perhaps even negated by the implications of sexual violence so nearby.

Linked together and viewed in a contemporary light, these images that Bierk has juxtaposed do not propose an easy answer to any problems. They do impose and assert a powerful presence, and while this is a challenge to the viewer, Bierk also intends to offer a sanctuary for reflection. – D.S.

A Eulogy to Art,

Interior (Le viol),

to Degas and Fantin-Latour

oil on canvas, oil on plaster

on plywood, wood, gold leaf

86" x 194½"

1992

Collection: Art Gallery of Peterborough,

Peterborough, Ont.

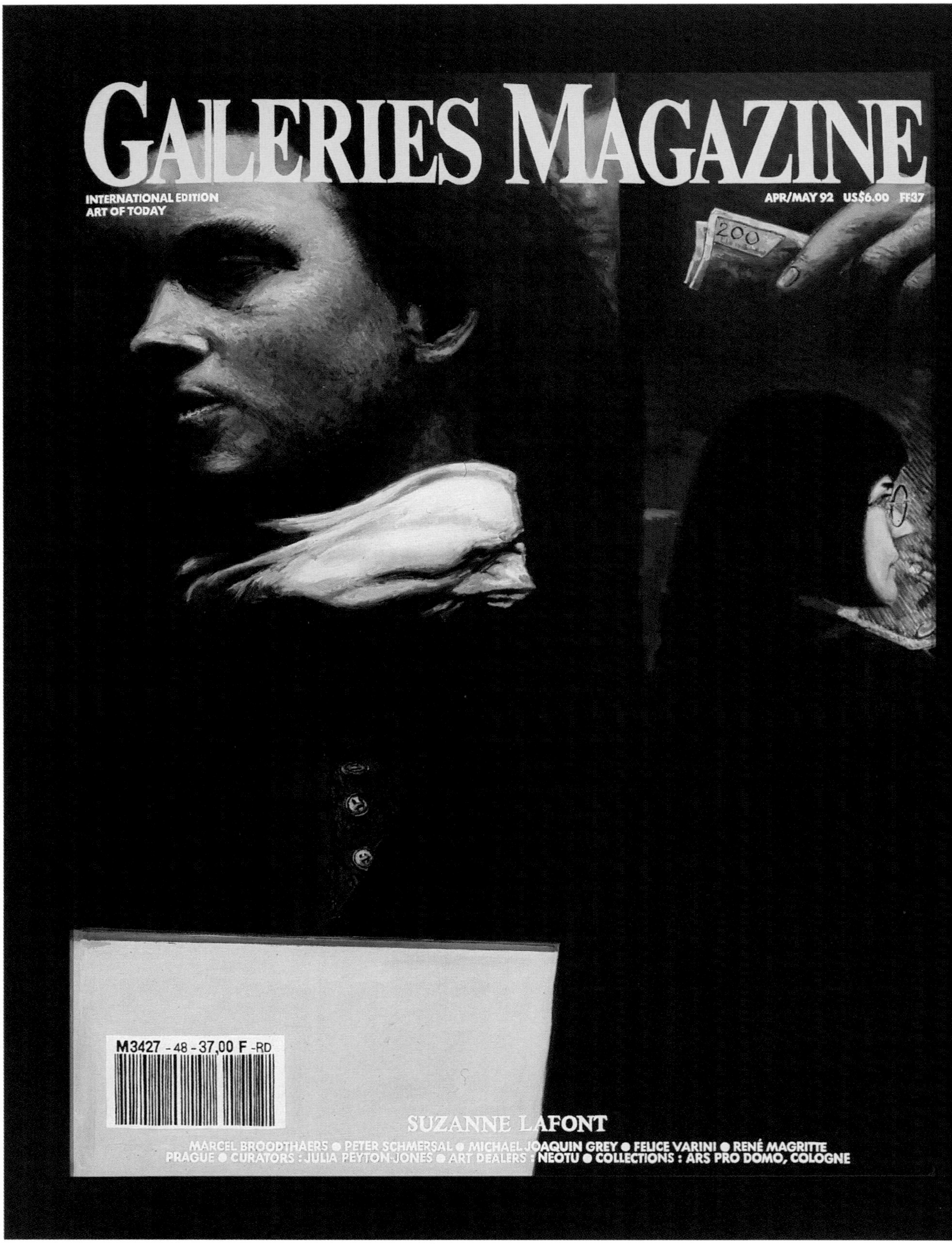

GALERIES MAGAZINE
INTERNATIONAL EDITION
ART OF TODAY
APR/MAY 92 US$6.00 FF37
200
M3427 - 48 - 37,00 F -RD
SUZANNE LAFONT
MARCEL BROODTHAERS ● PETER SCHMERSAL ● MICHAEL JOAQUIN GREY ● FELICE VARINI ● RENÉ MAGRITTE
PRAGUE ● CURATORS : JULIA PEYTON-JONES ● ART DEALERS : NEOTU ● COLLECTIONS : ARS PRO DOMO, COLOGNE

Preceding page:

An Allegory of Balance –

to Vermeer and Suzanne Lafont

oil on canvas

40" x 68"

1993

Collection: Perry Wolfman,

Toronto, Ont.

Above:

Approaching the 21st Century –

An Allegory of Balance –

to Lorrain and Mantegna

oil on canvas, photo by W. Wilson,

steel

69" x 193"

1993

The first major landscape painting I produced was commissioned by the Government of Ontario for a new Ministry of Health building in Kingston, Ontario, in 1983. For the past few years I had been working on the 'Canadian Rock Series' from photographs of rock outcroppings, but this commission involved a specific site (the Kingston Locks) as subject matter. As I had never previously painted a traditional landscape from nature, this was a huge challenge. I remember driving to the site and walking past the man-made intrusion of the locks and exploring the river and surrounding woods. It was exactly like walking into a sublime landscape of Caspar David Friedrich's or into a romantic Hudson River landscape.

In California, when I was growing up, painting the landscape was a taboo for any serious painter. This was in part because historically many artists has already painted it so beautifully, and also because the California topography had been over-marketed in the media and in the process had become a

clichéd image, especially in the art world. And so, when the Kingston commission came about, a whole new subject matter was opened up to me. The finished work was framed with a series of smaller landscapes tracing the history of that genre, beginning what was to become my ongoing exploration of landscape in both paint and photography.

Shortly after completing the commission I began work on a body of small paintings called 'The Save the Planet Imaginary

Far left:

Untitled

(in progress)

oil on canvas,

oil on board

8' x 12'

1985

Collection: Government of Ontario, Canada

Centre:

Distant Light: Black Chinese Vase, to Constable

oil on canvas

72" x 108"

1989

Below:

Summer Storm, Radium Rain

oil on board

31" x 37½"

1991

Private collection

Landscape Series' which portrayed the landscape both as a symbol of pure nature and as a cultural icon. This series launched what remains an important direction in my work. Today, as then, the landscape is a vehicle of expression for my political and ecological concerns. The sources for these works are my imagination, historical landscapes, my own photographs or sometimes a combination of all three. I consider my landscapes to be the heart of my creative output. – D.B.

The Dayton Art Institute exhibition, 'In the Absence of Paradise: Paintings by David Bierk', 1993, was the culmination of a series of exhibitions of my work under the 'absence of paradise' title. The exhibition was designed as an in-depth survey of the work I had produced since my departure from Artspace, covering the period from 1987 to 1991. While the inaugural exhibition at the Art Gallery of Peterborough also included a number of my earlier works, subsequent exhibitions grew to include more recent work. In addition to the Art Gallery of Peterborough and the Dayton Art Institute the exhibition travelled to the Ottawa Art Gallery, the University of Waterloo Art Gallery, and to Rodman Hall and the Niagara Artists Centre in St. Catharines, Ontario. – D.B.

Still-life paintings customarily express notions of life's fleeting beauty, a reminder that life is short and beauty is temporal. While still celebrating the richness and fecundity of organic life, a still-life painting produces meaning by way of allegory. Viewed in this mode, flowers are regenerative symbols of life and at the same time are memorials to the decay of beauty.

The old Dutch paintings which are sources for some of Bierk's latest paintings are works from an art history that was highly moral, expressive of and sensitive to beauty. For us these works are located wistfully in the past (that is, absent in the present). The melancholy of these quotes from art history speaks to the perceived decay of the present time, the absence of passion, a sense of fading light. Simultaneously, in the juxtapo-sition of the still lifes with images of contemporary art magazine covers, such as *Artforum/Still Life (An Allegory of Balances) to Hamilton and Jan van Huysum,* Bierk critiques the poverty of the present art scene and looks at parallels between art and life, then and now. And yet Bierk insists that his choice to re-present these lush and beautiful works is a statement of faith which implies there is *still* life – in people and the condition of this planet. With vigour and enthusiasm, Bierk is passionately recalling his themes of a eulogy for past values and the opti-mistic recovery of art history, resulting in a group of paintings which which are exquisitely beautiful and at the same time powerfully contemporary. – D.S.

Centre:
Artforum/Still Life
(An Allegory of Balances) to Hamilton and Jan van Huysum
oil on canvas
61½" x 108½"
1994

Below, left:
Still life study,
after Maria van Oosterwijk
oil on gold leaf on canvas
23" x 23"
1994
Collection: External Affairs and International Trade Canada, Ottawa, Ont.

Below, right:
Still life study,
after Abraham Mignon
oil on gold leaf on canvas
23" x 23"
1994
Collection: External Affairs and International Trade Canada, Ottawa, Ont.

DAVID BIERK

A FICTITIOUS FILM IN PROGRESS

by Gary Michael Dault

> … THE AIR WE FIND IN THE OLD MASTERS' PICTURES IS NOT THE AIR WE BREATHE.
> — EDGAR DEGAS

[THIS MELTS AWAY AS THE BLACKNESS GIVES WAY TO THE LIGHT-FILLED INTERIOR OF THE ARTIST'S STUDIO; SHAFTS OF SUNLIGHT SLANT DOWN INTO THE ROOM, FALLING AT LAST UPON THE FACE OF A CANVAS ON WHICH THERE IS A PICTURE IN PROGRESS. WE SEE THE ARTIST'S HAND WIELDING A LOADED BRUSH; WE HEAR THE ROUGHNESS AND THE RASPING AS THE PIGMENT IS SCUMBLED EXPERTLY ONTO THE FEATURES OF ONE OF THE NOBLE ITALIAN YOUTHS CONGREGATING WITH HIS FELLOWS IN A PAINTING BY MANTEGNA. WE KNOW THE FACE OF THIS YOUTH IS FROM A PAINTING BY MANTEGNA BECAUSE JUST AT THIS MOMENT, THE CAMERA PULLS BACK AND SPREADS OUT SUFFICIENTLY THAT WE CAN *NOW* SEE THAT THE PAINTER IS USING AS HIS MODEL (AS IT WERE) A REPRODUCTION OF A SHARD OF A PAINTING BY MANTEGNA AS IT APPEARS IN A CERTAIN ISSUE OF *FMR* MAGA-ZINE – WHICH IS PROPPED UP BEFORE THE PAINTER AS DELIBERATELY AND AS REVERENTLY AS ANOTHER ARTIST MIGHT HAVE ARRANGED A BOWL OF FRUIT BEFORE A GENERALIZING SCRIM OF CRUSHED VELVET. THE CAMERA RETURNS ONCE AGAIN TO THE CLOSE-UP CONSIDERATION OF THE PAINTERLY MODELING OF THE VISAGE OF THE MANTEGNA-YOUTH. THE ROUGH AND SCUMBLE OF THE PAINTING SESSION CONTINUES ON THE SCREEN, OVER WHICH WE HEAR …]

NARRATOR (V/O):

There is a story in Jorge Luis Borges' *Ficciones* which may contribute something emblematic to an understanding of the meaning of David Bierk's work. The story is called *Pierre Menard, Author of Don Quixote*, and involves some analysis of a writer who, according to Borges, sets out in the early years of this century to write the ninth and the thirty-eighth chapters of Part One of *Don Quixote* and a fragment of the twenty-second chapter. This, Borges points out quickly and earnestly, is no merely absurd matter of *copying out* Cervantes, nor is it a matter of transporting Cervantes' tenacious hero into the present ('Don Quixote on Wall Street') – thus evoking what Borges dyspeptically refers to as that 'plebeian delight in anachronism'. Rather, Borges' writer 'Pierre Menard' intends (his intention is 'merely astonishing'), by means of an epic immersion in the world and the mind of Cervantes, *to become* that earlier writer so entirely that the strangely holographic reappearance (of *Don Quixote*) will occur 'naturally' … [WE HEAR THE RUCKUS OF DAVID BIERK'S LOADED BRUSH; THE SOUND EDDIES UP FOR A MOMENT LIKE A VORTEX OF DRY LEAVES LIFTED BY A LITTLE TWISTER OF WIND AND THEN RELEASED AGAIN.] 'I have contracted the mysterious duty of reconstructing literally his [i.e. Cervantes'] spontaneous

■ David's *Mantegna*

■ Source image for David's *Mantegna* as reproduced in *FMR*

■ *FMR*

work', writes Menard to the admiring Borges. 'My solitary game is governed by two polar laws. The first permits me to attempt variants of a formal and psychological nature; the second obliges me to sacrifice them to the "original" text and irrefutably to rationalize this annihilation ... ' The result of Menard's extraordinary labours, according to Borges, is that 'the fragmentary Don Quixote of Menard is more subtle than that of Cervantes ... '

[WHAT FOLLOWS IS THROWN LIKE A PROJECTION UPON THE STUDIO INTERIOR IN WHICH DAVID BIERK IS LABOURING AWAY AT HIS MANTEGNA. THE WORDS FLOW UP OVER THE PAINTING SESSION AS A CONVENTIONAL 'EXPLANATION' SO OFTEN USED IN FILM TO ESTABLISH AN HISTORICAL CONTEXT FOR THE ACTION THAT IS TO FOLLOW. THE NARRATOR READS IT AS IT ROLLS UP AND AWAY.]

'The text of Cervantes and that of Menard are verbally identical', writes Borges, 'but the second is almost infinitely richer. (More ambiguous, his detractors will say; but ambiguity is a richness.)' Then there are comparisons. Here, for example, is Cervantes:

   ... TRUTH, WHOSE MOTHER IS HISTORY, WHO IS THE RIVAL OF TIME, DEPOSITORY OF DEEDS, WITNESS OF THE PAST, EXAMPLE AND LESSON TO THE PRESENT, AND WARNING TO THE FUTURE.

Written in the seventeenth century, written by the 'ingenious layman' Cervantes, this enumeration is a mere rhetorical eulogy of history. Menard, on the other hand, writes:

   ... TRUTH, WHOSE MOTHER IS HISTORY, WHO IS THE RIVAL OF TIME, DEPOSITORY OF DEEDS, WITNESS OF THE PAST, EXAMPLE AND LESSON TO THE PRESENT, AND WARNING TO THE FUTURE.

History, mother of truth; the idea is astounding. Menard, a contemporary of William James, does not define history as an investigation of reality, but as its origin. Historical truth, for him, is not what took place; it is what we think took place. The final clauses – *example and lesson to the present, and warning to the future* – are shamelessly pragmatic ... And so Borges finds the

■ *Approaching the 21st Century/An Allegory of Balances/to Lorrain and Mantegna*
  oil on canvas, photo by W. Wilson, steel, 69" x 193", 1993

■ *Mantegna* reproduction, *FMR*
■ David at work on his *Mantegna*

Menard *Don Quixote* the more compelling of the two, even though Menard's Spanish is slightly 'archaic', compared to the way Cervantes himself handles the 'ordinary Spanish of his time'. It must be understood that Menard has not fabricated a mere *gloss* on the Cervantes original text. But what he *has* done, in many complex ways, is comment on the fact of the earlier (and 'authentic') work. This reenactment – rebirth, in essence – lies, as a paradigm, somewhere *beyond* the slightly dandified realms of mere appropriation.

[HAVING SAID AS MUCH, THE SUPERIMPOSED CRAWL OF TEXT FINISHES ITS CLIMB TO THE TOP OF THE SCREEN AND DISAPPEARS. WE ARE LEFT ALONE IN THE STUDIO WITH DAVID BIERK AND HIS LOADED BRUSH AND THE MANTEGNA QUOTATION BLOOMING BENEATH HIS

MINISTRATIONS. THE MANTEGNA FACE BIERK IS PAINTING BLEEDS THROUGH TO DAVID'S OWN FACE. HE ADDRESSES THE CAMERA DIRECTLY.]

DAVID BIERK [TO CAMERA]:
We moved to California when I was a child, after my father and mother were divorced. My mother is an incredible person. She was very strong and unselfish bringing me up on her own, earning a living for the two of us, moving us to Lafayette so that I could go to a really good school. We were plunked into an upper middle class neighbourhood before divorce was common, and she not only provided for me but was my mother, father, teacher and friend. I look back and think what a courageous thing to do. It was my uncle Spiros, though, who taught me – at an early age – what you might call the work ethic. I always worked, at least from the time I was in grade six or seven. Spiros was unbelievably *dynamic* and became a sort of father figure to me. He owned a mayonnaise factory in San Francisco and I started working there, doing things like scraping the labels off returned mayonnaise bottles and scraping the mold from

■ David and mother, Yosemite, 1956   ■ Studio panorama

cheese … I'd be working eight-hour days in the summers from the time I was 12 or 13.

OFF-CAMERA INTERVIEWER:

It all sounds very *Horatio Alger*-like. From just such a humble forge is the American Dream generated, is it not?

DAVID BIERK:

Well, I was learning self-reliance, for sure. While all the other kids were *given* their first cars during high school, for example, I saved for one from what I earned by working, and eventually bought a 1956 Chev for twelve hundred dollars.

INTERVIEWER:

You were sort of an *American Graffiti* kid?

DAVID BIERK:

Funny you should put it that way. *American Graffiti* – the film – depicted teenage life in 1962, the year I graduated from high school. I think it was filmed in Fresno. I was sort of a knock-about kid. I goofed off all the time … off to the beach with a case of beer. Listen, I was probably the most popular kid in my high school. I had this nickname: 'Hondo'. All that is one of the reasons I can understand Sebastian.

[QUICK SHOT OF SEBASTIAN BACH, LEAD SINGER OF THE AMERICAN HEAVY METAL GROUP *SKID ROW* – CLOSE-UP PHOTO OF SEBASTIAN ON THE COVER OF *ROLLING STONE* MAGAZINE (SEPTEMBER 1991). THIS PHOTO IS THEN COVERED BY A BLOWUP OF A NEWSPAPER HEAD-LINE (*THE PETERBOROUGH EXAMINER*, DECEMBER 21, 1987) READING 'ROCK CAREER FOR YOUNGER BIERK'.]

INTERVIEWER:

Sebastian Bach is Sebastian Bierk – your son?

DAVID BIERK [GRINNING DELIGHTEDLY]:

That's right. [THE MUSIC OF SKID ROW ENGULFS THE CONVERSATION AND THE SCREEN FADES TO BLACK.]

[FOCUS ON THE LURID, BLOOD-RED OPEN WOUND THAT IS THE NAME 'SKID ROW'. THE CAMERA PULLS BACK AND WE SEE THAT THE NAME IS PAINTED ON A CANVAS. AS THE CAMERA CONTINUES TO PULL BACK, WE ARE ABLE TO TAKE IN THE WHOLE PAINTING – AN ENORMOUS, MURAL-SIZE PANORAMIC EPIC 6 FEET BY 16 FEET. THE CAMERA DRIFTS ALONG

■ David's Uncle Spiros
■ David, Oakland, 1964

97

ITS GREAT LENGTH AND WE INSPECT ITS SURFACE, NOTING THE GREEN-GOLD SKIES, THE DISPOSITION OF THE FIGURES (OF WHICH THERE SEEM TO BE HUNDREDS). AS THE CAMERA CONTINUES ITS SLOW SWEEP, WE HEAR THE VOICE OF DAVID BIERK TALKING ABOUT THE PICTURE.]

DAVID BIERK (V/O):

The picture is based on a work by Caravaggio, depicting the burial of St. Lucia. There are two muscular goons in the foreground digging her grave. Here, for use as the cover art for Skid Row's second album, *Slave to the Grind*, I have replaced the dead saint with a more or less sacrificial young man, a rock musician, so that the picture is both a eulogy for a young man the band knew who died and also, at a more general level, the endangered spirit of rock and roll being buried by technology and hype and lethal glamour. Some of the characters are from Caravaggio's era, while others [WE SEE THEM] are from our own time – John F. Kennedy, for example, and a policeman and a heavy-metal 'moll' ... and of course amid the historically positioned details are strewn modern-day moments: a TV, hypodermic needles – that kind of thing – all pressed densely into this more or less conventionalized context.

■ Album cover painting being lowered from David's studio

■ Billboard at Tower Records, Los Angeles, Calif.

■ Caravaggio's *The Burial of St. Lucia*, 1608-9

OFF-SCREEN INTERVIEWER:

This is an enormously complex work – and demanding, I should think. How long were you engaged in painting it?

DAVID BIERK [LAUGHING]:

A week and a half. [LAUGHTER IN THE STUDIO, FROM CREW AND INTERVIEWER]

INTERVIEWER:

How long would a picture this size normally take you?

DAVID BIERK:

Normally, it would take – I'd like to have taken – about three months. But I just didn't have it. Instead I worked at the painting 'round the clock, 12 to 14 hours a day ...

INTERVIEWER:

Just as well that Uncle Spiros taught you the heady joys of hard work!

DAVID BIERK:

For sure. And I'm happiest working that way too. Actually it was great – very theatrical. With the help of a local theatre group here in Peterborough, we filled the studio night after night with real-life models for the figures in the painting. We had about seventy-five people running around in here, everyone from naked babies to older people, some dressed in period costume and some in modern dress ... it was like the opening night of a play that never opened. I just painted right through it. A number of the people who posed for the painting are recognizable as themselves: here, for example, are my other sons [WE FIND THEM IN THE PAINTING] – here's Zac ... and Alex ... Jeff ... and Nicholas ... And here is one of the invaluable people I employ to help me in the studio, Pablo Ridley.

INTERVIEWER:

Is Sebastian there somewhere?

DAVID BIERK:

No. None of Skid Row themselves are here. [WE FOCUS IN TIGHT ON THE PAINTING AGAIN AND THE MUSIC OF SKID ROW ENGULFS THE IMAGE, FORCING US TO FADE TO BLACK.]

[SCENE: THE MAIN STREET OF PETERBOROUGH, ONTARIO, THE PRETTY, SOMNOLENT LITTLE CITY WHERE BIERK HAS LIVED FOR THE PAST TWENTY-ONE YEARS. WE ACCOMPANY BIERK ON A STROLL ALONG THE STREET – A STROLL WHICH WILL LEAD FINALLY TO HIS STUDIO.]

THEY SAID IT COULD NOT BE DONE. CHALLENGE THE MUSIC INDUSTRY'S PERCEPTION OF A 'GOOD' ALBUM COVER? BRIDGE THE GENERATION GAP BETWEEN HEAVY METAL AND MODERN ART? MIX BUSINESS WITH FAMILY? MIX SKID ROW WITH CARAVAGGIO? THEY SAID IT COULD NOT BE DONE …

After a first album with great tunes and a good (i.e. clichéd) cover, we knew that things were going to be different the second time around. After seeing my father's work, our band and management decided to approach him about making the heaviest cover of all time. Of course my Dad did just that.

Upon its release in 1991, *Slave to the Grind* debuted at number one on *Billboard Magazine's* top LP chart, the first album to do so since Michael Jackson's *Bad*. The album cover itself was acclaimed as number one – best of the year – by trade magazines in Japan, Sweden, the U.K., the U.S.A., and Canada. It was also voted fifth best album cover of 1991 by the readership of *Rolling Stone* magazine and ranked ninth best cover of all time in a 1992 *Circus Magazine*.

THEY SAID IT COULD NOT BE DONE. RIGHT ON, DAD. – Sebastian Bierk

■ *Slave to the Grind (Skid Row album cover)*, oil on canvas, 6' x 16', 1991

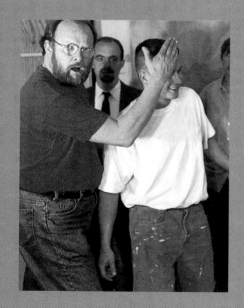

■ David directing the album cover photo session

■ Photo sources for the album cover

I remember
a Planet of the Apes comic book
salt and vinegar chips
the crumbs falling off my fingers
and freezing into the zipper
of my jacket

the snow is piled high
and the bottom of it is
greasy blue black
the sound of the
Canadian Tires
on George Street at 7 a.m.

And we're off to Madoc
for the day
to transport art
and read
and listen to the radio

– Sebastian Bierk

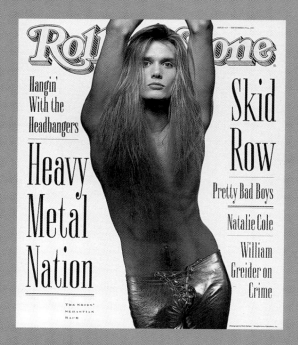

■ Sebastian on the cover of *Rolling Stone* magazine
■ David working on the prototype for the album cover

99

DAVID BIERK [TO UNSEEN INTERVIEWER]:

Thinking about it now, it was an incredible time to be growing up in California with the issues of free speech, black power and the war in Vietnam in my own back yard, so to speak. But I was more interested in baseball and my car and the head cheerleader and it wasn't until later, when I traded in my glove for a paint brush, that I began to consider those influences seriously. I joined the National Guard after high school and ended up at the California College of Arts and Crafts in Oakland, where I forced myself to endure its very traditional approach to painting instruction when all I wanted was to be given a blank canvas ...

INTERVIEWER:

Did any of your teachers make a contribution to your understanding of art?

DAVID BIERK:

Yes. I took an English Literature course – just on my own – from Michael McClure, the beat poet who wrote *Scratching the Beat Surface*. He was an influence, in the sense that he made it clear that there was 'a different way' to do things, see things. But in retrospect that technical teaching I received at Arts & Crafts has proven to be the foundation of the craft side of my art. That was extremely useful. And then after about a year and a half as an art student I took off ...

INTERVIEWER:

Where to?

DAVID BIERK:

I hitchhiked across the country ... ended up in Florida. From there I caught a boat over to the Bahamas ...

INTERVIEWER [INCREDULOUS]:

The Bahamas? Why?

DAVID BIERK [AMUSED]:

I don't know. It was partly the Easy Rider thing. I wanted to see what was beyond Lafayette, California. Mostly, too, I think because I thought I could get a job there. I figured I'd be a lifeguard ... stretched out all day beneath the sheltering palms, ready to leap to the assistance of bronzed maidens in distress ... none of which happened, of course. It was romantic, though; the absolute antithesis of my life growing up in the rather conservative world of Lafayette, California. There were discos on the beach – I saw George Hamilton on the beach one day!

INTERVIEWER [LAUGHS]:

Gee!

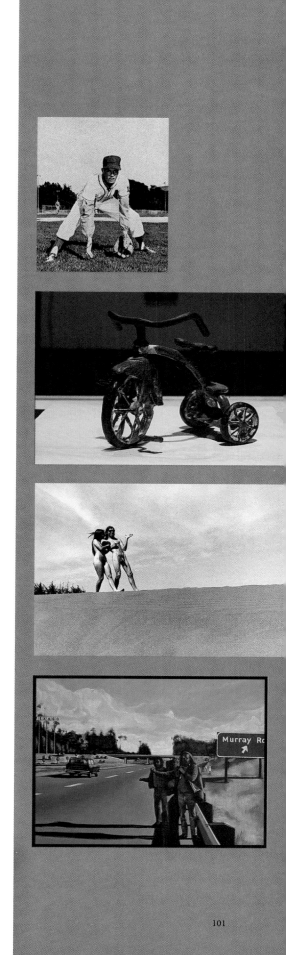

- David at age 16, 1960
- *Tricycle,* enamel on bronze, 6" high, 1965
- *Friends Series: Trucking for Peace,* tinted photomontage, 8" x 12", 1972
- *Hitchhiker,* oil on canvas, 4' x 6', 1976. Private collection

DAVID BIERK [ENJOYING THIS]:

Yeah! But, you know, a number of *really important things* happened to me there. For example, I *did* get a job there, though it wasn't as a lifeguard. [BY THIS TIME WE ARE OUTSIDE DAVID BIERK'S STUDIO ON GEORGE STREET. HE OPENS THE DOOR AND WE CLIMB THE STAIRS TO THE THIRD FLOOR. WE ENTER THE STUDIO.]

DAVID BIERK [CONTINUING]:

What I got was a job at the sublimely named Mary Star of the Sea School – which was, of course, a Catholic grammar school. What they were looking for was a librarian. I didn't have any idea how to be a librarian. So I phoned my mother in Lafayette to send me a user's manual to the Dewey decimal system and, armed with that, got the job. The school was in Freeport. And – more's the miracle – we actually put together a good little library, too! Sister Mary Alice, who had hired me, was very pleased. The importance of all this is that I persuaded Sister Mary Alice to let me *teach art* as well, which she did. And which I found, to my surprise, I could do very well – and also found, to my surprise, I enjoyed a great deal. [CLOSE-UP OF FADED NEWSPAPER PHOTO OF DAVID BIERK AND SELECTED STUDENTS STANDING EXCITEDLY AMONG AMBITIOUS ART PROJECTS.] ... [BACK TO THE PRESENT, DAVID BIERK IN STUDIO.]

■ David, friends and family in the Bahamas, 1967-71

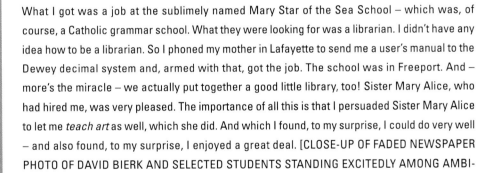

102

DAVID BIERK [MUSING]:

I don't really believe in *luck* … but I think I *do* believe in *fate*.

INTERVIEWER:

And hard work?

DAVID BIERK:

Lots of that. That's a given. But *fate*, yes. Being open to allow things to happen. I've always felt this way and worked hard. I think this is where it all came from …

DAVID BIERK:

Where *what* all came from?

DAVID BIERK [MAKING AN INCLUSIVE GESTURE WITH HIS HAND, REACHING OUT TO DRAW INTO HIS EMBRACE ALL OF THE LIFE OF HIS ART STACKED AROUND HIM IN THE STUDIO (WHICH IS ALIVE NOW WITH ACTIVITY, STUDIO ASSISTANTS SCURRYING ABOUT, FRAMING BEING DONE IN AN ADJOINING SHOP, ETC.)]:

Everything. All this. Who I am. What I do. I don't know. It just began to occur to me in the Bahamas that you could just do pretty much anything you wanted to do, as long as [SMILES AT THE REMEMBRANCE] you *never stopped doing it.* [PHOTOGRAPHS COME AND GO BEFORE THE CAMERA, ONE BLEEDING INTO ANOTHER.]

[CUT TO A SLIDE LECTURE IN PROGRESS. CRITIC GARY MICHAEL DAULT IS DISCUSSING DAVID BIERK'S WORK BEFORE WHAT WE SENSE – THOUGH WE CANNOT SEE IT – IS A LARGE AND ENTHUSIASTIC CROWD. THE CAMERA STAYS ON DAULT AND THE GIANT PROJECTED IMAGE BEHIND HIM.]

GARY MICHAEL DAULT [MID-LECTURE]:

… the point being that within the range of appropriative procedures, the *Slave to the Grind* painting, done for the Skid Row CD – not the least of its appeals being the poignant *futility* of its elephantine scale, considering that what was *required* was a painting six inches square for the CD package – the *Slave to the Grind* painting *does* partake of what Jorge Luis Borges in his story 'Pierre Menard, Author of Don Quixote' in *Ficciones* refers to as 'a plebeian delight in anachronism' (appropriate enough, given its probable audience), whereas a more 'serious' painting of the same period, a work like [THE SLIDE CHANGES SO THAT WE ARE NOW GAZING UPON IT] *In the Absence of Virtue, Art in America, May 1990, to J.L. David and Manet* (1990) depends, for the complex net of meanings it throws up, upon a purer, more *raw* kind of juxtaposition that admits

■ Peterborough studio (3)

■ *In the Absence of Virtue, Art in America, May 1990, to J.L. David and Manet*, oil on canvas, oil on plaster on plywood, 44½" x 74", 1990

103

of none of the kind of chronological game-playing that lends the *Skid Row* painting its energy. Here, the preoccupations are quite different ... [THE LECTURE CONTINUES, BUT GROWS DISTANT AS WE PULL AWAY AND BLEED INTO THE NEXT SCENE...WHICH TAKES US TO DAVID BIERK'S HOME ON A COOL, TREE-LINED STREET IN PETERBOROUGH. WE ARE IN THE BACK YARD, BESIDE THE POOL. THERE ARE A FEW FRIENDS GATHERED HERE; DAVID BIERK'S WIFE LIZ SITS LISTENING TO THE PROCEEDINGS. HIS CHILDREN PLAY NEARBY. THE NARRATOR REMAINS OFF-SCREEN AND BIERK ADDRESSES HIS REMARKS TO HIM, AND THUS TO THE CAMERA.]

DAVID BIERK:

I stayed in the Bahamas for two years, and it was *there* that I decided to make art the focus of my life. So when I returned to California I went back to school – art school. Because I was really serious now about art, I deliberately chose a school away from what I saw as the temptations of Southern California, and ended up at Humboldt State University (which was part of the University of California) in the northern part of the state, about 60 miles from the Oregon border. And *there* [LAUGHS] I adopted a *serious* attitude for the first time. I really *wanted* to learn how to paint and how to become a teacher (thinking, at that point, that there was some way to *learn* this). It was really a good atmosphere for me, and it became a sort of alternative place, too, for this whole Haight-Ashbury movement. Arcata, for example, was the site of a sort of tense but energetic standoff between the rednecks who had always lived there and the war protesters who found their way there. [MUSIC UNDER: PERIOD CALIFORNIA ROCK. CUT TO CLOSE-UP OF INTERVIEWER'S NOTEBOOK: HE HAS JUST SCRIBBLED ON ONE OF ITS PAGES

■ Outside David's Arcata, Calif. studio, 1971

■ Younger Bierk children, 1994

■ *American Youth Series: The Cardplayers*, oil on canvas, 8' x 18', 1969
  Collection: Humboldt State University, Arcata, Calif.

'Beginning of dichotomy idea in Bierk's paintings? Diptych might come out of juxtaposition of cultural styles?']

DAVID BIERK (V/O):

I remember, in Marin County, being passed by a sinister old Chrysler Imperial. The entire top had been torched off so it was like a kind of demented, crazed convertible, and there were ten or twelve people crushed into it. On the hood they had bolted this ersatz creature – Marvin the Wonder Horse. I was delirious with change and with issues and ideas. I felt like Marvin. It really was like being the hood ornament of popular culture – being in California then, I mean. Everything happened there first.

[CUT TO DAULT SLIDE LECTURE STILL IN PROGRESS. THE GIANT IMAGE ON THE SCREEN IS DAVID BIERK'S *IN SEARCH OF THE AMERICAN DREAM* FROM 1971. VISUALLY, THE EFFECT IS DISCONCERTING, IN THAT IT TAKES A SECOND OR SO TO PEEL BACK THE LAYERINGS OF THE SCENE: IN THE FOREGROUND, DAULT AT THE MICROPHONE.]

GARY MICHAEL DAULT [MID-LECTURE]:

... so that the final effect of the Shirley Temple image, the twinkling child star with, in Bierk's treatment, the almost savagely white teeth and the preternaturally dancing eyes – which hiss and spark like a lit fuse – is that of a *great towering mushroom cloud of a film star* (the painting is 24 feet high) blocking out the otherwise pastoral sky. This is something the viewer, and only the viewer can see, however. The explosion of pop culture going on behind them is entirely unnoticed by the good, grey aggregate educators in the foreground. In this sense – as well as in a number of others – the painting is *prophetic*. It is also prophetic in a formal sense, of course, to the degree that it would underscore, for Bierk, the multi-valent usefulness of the idea of juxtaposition ...

DAVID BIERK [POOLSIDE]:

It was the *isolation* of being up north in California that was so important. I was painting ten to twelve hours a day, I was getting good grades at Humboldt, my daughter Heather was born there ... these were wonderful years for me, during this formative time. We lived on campus in an old

■ *Friends Series: Marvin the Wonder Horse*, tinted photomontage, 8" x 12", 1972
Collection: T. Pfliger, Kingston, Ont.

■ *Shirley Temple* painting, 1975

■ David with daughter, Heather, 1972

105

KRIZIA. Corpetto in lino blu, come la tuta annodata, con borchie in metallo. Accessori Krizia. Il servizio è stato realizzato grazie alla gentile collaborazione di "94th Aero Squadron", 1395 N.W. 57th Ave, Miami Florida 305-261-4220.

My ninth birthday present from my Dad was a trip to New York City to see the Broadway production of 'Annie'. That visit is still a vivid one to me – the lights of Times Square, my first crazy cab ride, and waiting anxiously at the stage door to get autographs from the cast. I also remember (as on most trips with my Dad) going from gallery to gallery in an area called 'Soho'. At one particular gallery Dad seemed to talk to the artist forever. I didn't mind because after Dad proudly introduced me, Joseph Rafael signed one of his beautiful colour postcards for me! During that trip, Dad not only spoiled me, his only daughter, on my ninth birthday but he also opened my eyes to the endless possibilities of the world beyond rural Ontario and the fourth grade! Ten years later Dad and I went to New York again. This time he was armed with slides of his latest work and I, a would-be model, with some photographs taken by dear old Dad. Although I'm sure that university was his first choice for my immediate future, Dad gave me the support and confidence I needed to hit those cold streets. And that's what we did – Dad to the galleries and I to modelling agencies. Little did we know what changes that week would bring. Dad signed with the Bess Cutler Gallery and I ended up staying in New York, having that same day been given a haircut, photo shoot and contract by Paris U.S.A., my new agency! That night we celebrated at my brother Bass' house. He had just received numerous awards including 'Singer of the Year' from *Metal Edge* magazine. It was quite a week! Since then I have travelled extensively, working in cities around the world. It is always the biggest thrill when Dad tells me to check out a gallery and I walk in and see his work. It's hard to describe, but the feeling is one of immense familiarity, inspiration and pride. – *Heather Bierk*

■ Heather in *Italia Harper's Bazaar*, 1993

Victorian house. My Master's thesis was to do enough work for a show and then install it — I suppose all this was good training for my eventual curatorial years at *Artspace* here in Peterborough. And, of course, I started to exhibit beyond the school too, in groups around the state. [ONE OF THE GUESTS ASKS IF TEACHING HASN'T ALWAYS BEEN AN *INTERFERENCE* IN BIERK'S LIFE AS A PAINTER.] The fact is, I always thought you had to teach; I thought *teaching* art was inextricably bound up with *making* art ...

[CUT TO GARY MICHAEL DAULT BEING HIMSELF QUESTIONED BY OFF-SCREEN INTERVIEWER. DAULT SITS ON A CHAIR FACING THE CAMERA.]

GARY MICHAEL DAULT:

... I think you could argue that David's current painting is still about *teaching*, to some extent ...

INTERVIEWER [OFF-SCREEN]:

Doesn't that end up relegating it to the realm of the didactic, if not the pedantic?

GARY MICHAEL DAULT:

Not in the least. Teaching is a mode by which the presentation and enactment of choice is liberating and expansive, not diminishing. It seems to me that a good deal of what goes on in David's painting addresses such issues as 'how do we *acquire*?' Within the diptych format itself, for example, lies a paradigm of the teaching mode of acquisition: what is to be acquired in this painting and is it *will or passivity* that informs the works? That is, do you simply allow both sides of the work entry, or do you not rather participate in some judgement about the power and relevance of the images one to the other and both of them in some triangulation involving you, the viewer?

■ (centre) *Aurora*, oil on canvas, 72" x 90", 1987
  Private collection

■ Graduate exhibition, Humboldt State University, Arcata, Calif., 1972

■ *American Youth Series: Dream Search*, oil and acrylic on canvas, 16' x 8', 1970. Collection: Brampton Public Library and Art Gallery, Brampton, Ont.

■ Graduate exhibition

[THE CAMERA PULLS BACK TO REVEAL THAT THE DAULT INTERVIEW HAS BEEN ON TAPE AND THAT WE HAVE BEEN WATCHING IT *WITHIN* OUR OWN FILM. A HAND NOW REACHES FOR THE MONITOR AND TURNS IT OFF. WE PULL BACK TO DISCOVER THAT WE ARE BACK IN DAVID BIERK'S STUDIO. IT WAS BIERK'S HAND THAT TURNED OFF THE VIDEOTAPE. HE CONTINUES TO ADDRESS AN OFF-CAMERA INTERVIEWER.]

DAVID BIERK:

… and so, naturally, I wanted a teaching job again; unfortunately, I wanted one at the same time as everyone else in the world wanted one. I ended up returning to the Bahamas for a brief period, but it wasn't any fun anymore – the country had gained independence while I was in California and, as a result, expatriates were no longer welcome … there was a general surliness afoot … there was nobody to talk to – I was twenty-four years old with two kids … The romance of the first time there was gone. So there I sat in the inhospitable Bahamas sending out résumés – I sent out four hundred and sixty-eight of them! There were a couple of possibilities in Canada, but what it came down to – in 1971 – was a virtual post-draft-dodger moratorium on hiring Americans. My sister-in-law lived in Toronto, so we moved there for a visit while I looked for work. En route, I met a city planner in Montreal who told me I had to go and see Av Isaacs in Toronto. Av was the very first person I spoke to on my arrival. While there I familiarized myself with the gallery scene in Toronto [WE SEE SHOTS OF THE TORONTO GALLERIES IN THOSE DAYS: THE ISAACS GALLERY, CARMEN LAMANNA, ETC. DAVID'S DISCUSSION IS V/O] – which struck me then as vibrant, pioneering, exploratory. One day, I spotted an ad in the *Globe and Mail* for a teaching job here in Peterborough. It was mid-August and we drove up here to look around [FOOTAGE OF PETERBOROUGH AT ITS MOST LAMBENT AND SEDUCTIVE] in a rented car – and, predictably, fell in love with the place. I got the job, too, which was convenient – at Kenner Collegiate.

OFF-SCREEN INTERVIEWER:

So how was that, teaching art in a high school in a small town in Ontario? Wasn't it a little confining?

DAVID BIERK [CHEERFULLY]:

On the contrary, it was a terrific two years. Maybe I wouldn't have enjoyed it so much if it had been a better located, better behaved high school. My first year there I had a classroom full of real juvenile delinquents. I remember showing this film by Norman McLaren one afternoon and this one big kid was so disruptive, I picked him up and threw him through the screen.

OFF-SCREEN INTERVIEWER:

It sounds like performance art.

■ En route to the Bahamas

■ David lecturing, Art Gallery of Ontario's 'Artists with their Work' programme

■ Sir Sandford Fleming College student gallery

DAVID BIERK:

Maybe it does *now*. *Then*, it was just a fit of bad temper, in a genial sort of way. Anyway, the school supported me in this and I went on – and so did the class – to have a great time! We built a darkroom, developed and printed our own photographs, made great big paintings, it was just fine.

OFF-SCREEN INTERVIEWER:

Tim Rollins and K.O.S.?

DAVID BIERK [AMUSED]:

Almost.

OFF-SCREEN INTERVIEWER:

And so you stayed in Peterborough, Ontario?

DAVID BIERK:

Yes. And I kept teaching, first at Kenner and then at Sir Sandford Fleming Community College where I probably could have stayed on and acquired tenure and settled down …

OFF-SCREEN INTERVIEWER:

And instead?

DAVID BIERK:

And instead I taught at the College for about 5 years before taking on *Artspace* full-time.

OFF-SCREEN INTERVIEWER:

Gee, there's job security for you! From a nice cozy college job to the directorship of an alternative gallery space in a small city north of Toronto.

■ (centre) The first *Artspace*, 440 Water St.

■ David and Liz, 190 Hunter St. *Artspace*

■ Larry Gray's *Inflatable Locomotive*, 'Monument to Miniature' exhibition, 1975, Peterborough, Ont.

DAVID BIERK:

Well, you make it sound purgatorial.

OFF-SCREEN INTERVIEWER:

And it wasn't?

DAVID BIERK:

Well, despite my respect for teaching, it became clear to me that you cannot be a full-time teacher and a serious painter at the same time.

OFF-SCREEN INTERVIEWER:

But you can be a serious painter and a full-time art gallery director and curator, right?

DAVID BIERK:

You have a better shot, yes.

[CUT TO FILM FOOTAGE OF THE MAIN STREET OF PETERBOROUGH, ONTARIO, OVER WHICH IS CUED THE TITLE *THE ARTSPACE YEARS*; WE REALIZE THAT WHAT WE ARE SEEING IS A MINI-DOCUMENTARY IMBEDDED IN THE LARGER ONE. HERE, IN A SWIFT ELISION OF IMAGES AND VOICES, WE ARE GIVEN SOME ENTRY TO THE DEMENTED CREATIVE FERMENT OF THE 13 YEARS BIERK SPENT WITH ARTSPACE, THE BEWILDERINGLY JOYOUS MOUNTING OF A CORNUCOPIA OF EXHIBITIONS AND PROJECTS AND PRODUCTION, SOME FRAGRANCE OF THE GENUINENESS WITH WHICH ARTSPACE SEEMED TO FEEL THAT NOTHING WAS ALIEN TO IT.]

[THIS IS THE SCREEN. WATCHING IT NOW YOU SEE INSTALLATION SHOTS OF EXHIBITIONS SUCH AS THE FAMOUS *MONUMENT TO MINIATURE* (WHICH FEATURED BIERK'S *IN SEARCH OF THE AMERICAN DREAM*), THE PARIS-BOUND *REFLECTING A RURAL CONSCIOUSNESS* (FOR THE CANADIAN CULTURAL CENTRE THERE), *THE GLASS SHOW*, ARTIST AND POET AND SOMETIME CHAIRMAN OF ARTSPACE *DENNIS TOURBIN* IN PERFORMANCE, THE ARTSPACE COUP OF GETTING THE WORLD-FAMOUS *CHRISTO* TO COME TO THE NOT-YET-WORLD-FAMOUS ARTSPACE FOR AN EXHIBITION AND LECTURE ('I JUST PICKED UP THE PHONE AND CALLED HIM,' EXPLAINS ARTSPACE'S DAVID BIERK). WE SEE THE ARTSPACE TRUCK WITH THE ASSEMBLED COMPLEMENT OF VOLUNTEER ASSISTANTS, WE WATCH FOOTAGE OF GALLERY RENOVATION, CULMINATING IN THE NOT INCONSIDERABLE TRIUMPH (IN 1984) OF SECURING THE CITY'S HANDSOME AND HISTORICALLY SIGNIFICANT MARKET HALL AS THE NEW ARTSPACE ART CENTRE (HEADLINE: 'THE RENOVATION OF THE MARKET HALL IS THE SINGLE MOST IMPORTANT HOPE THE CITY HAS FOR REVITALIZING THE DOWNTOWN CORE' – *THE PETERBOROUGH EXAMINER*, MAY 16, 1984). THE MINI-DOC FINISHES WITH FOOTAGE OF

■ John Boyle with his tepee, 'Refecting a Rural Consciousness' exhibition, Canadian Cultural Centre, Paris, 1980

■ Bierk and Christo at the Peterborough Liftlocks

■ Dennis Tourbin

THAT TRIUMPHANT NIGHT – STUDDED WITH STARS OF GOVERNMENT AND PURVEYORS OF FINANCIAL SUPPORT – WHEN THE NEW ARTSPACE OFFICIALLY OPENS; DAVID BIERK'S TRIUMPHANT SPEECH, PART TENDERNESS, PART GRATITUDE, PART EPIC AMBITION. THE PERFUME OF BUREAUCRATIC APOTHEOSIS IN THE AIR. *GETTING SOMETHING DONE.* IT'S A MIRACLE, IS IT NOT?]

[FADE TO BLACK]

NARRATOR [V/O VISUALS]:

With his *Laundromat, Canadian Interior* from 1975, Bierk added a new dimension to his canon of juxtapositions: *virtuosity*. The painting, stiff and starchy with its burden of Photo-Realism, shows three hieratically-arranged figures [THE CAMERA PANS SLOWLY AND MEDITATIVELY OVER THE WORK] – presumably (but not inevitably) Bierk himself, his first wife Kathleen, and their then young son Sebastian. The three figures together produce a triangulated space in the upper half of the canvas (the parents gaze upon the child and the child gazes out of the canvas space to 'meet' the viewer's returning inspection). This triangulated wedge, cut from the fictional family-space of the canvas, is structurally echoed by the hovering presence in the lower half of the canvas of a meticulously recreated and alarmingly foreshortened reading of Jan van Eyck's *Madonna of Canon van der Paele*. The composition of the van Eyck is *essentially* that of the laun-dromat-content of the painting, the centrally located virgin and child being replaced entirely (an appropriate displacement for an age in which the window full of the clouds of unknowingness is a better event-horizon than a traditional image of veneration) by weather and the flanking wings full of adoring attendants replaced by watchful parents and (structurally) by the banalities of a row of dryers and a table for folding clothes. Whatever the picture's sociological thrust, however (is it a condemnation of the sensuous and spiritual diminishments of our time? Compare floors, for example, the tiles and the carpeting), the recreation of the van Eyck is so foregrounded, not just by placement but also by the theatricality of its labour-intensiveness, that the painting turns out *mostly* – perhaps this is hindsight talking – to be a declaration by the painter that he sees the whole province of art history as an image bank (Yeats' *spiritus mundi*) from which he feels free to draw. This painterly declaration fills the picture entirely (the laundromat can never reclaim our attention from the art-historical intrusion). This is an early step in the language and methodology

■ (centre) David at his easel, 1993

■ First version *Laundromat ...* painting, 1974

■ *Laundromat, Canadian Interior,*
  oil on canvas, 5' x 7', 1975
  Collection: Art Gallery of Peterborough,
  Peterborough, Ont.

of the appropriation modality Bierk will explore and eventually (but not yet) bend to his own needs. At this point, he's just showing off. [TIGHT CLOSE-UP OF THE VAN EYCK FOLLOWED BY A BLEED-THROUGH TO DAVID BIERK'S STUDIO. BIERK'S FRIEND, POET AND PERFORMANCE ARTIST AND ARTSPACE ORGANIZER DENNIS TOURBIN, IS PERCHED ON A STOOL, ADDRESSING THE CAMERA DIRECTLY.]

DENNIS TOURBIN:

A few days later I visited David again in his studio. His young son Sebastian was reading an article from *artscanada* to him as he painted. I forget the title of the painting but I can see it clearly in my mind right now at this moment. *Sebastian was reading art history to David while David was painting.* That is a firm memory in my mind ... David set his brush down. Sebastian stopped reading and David smiled, completely aware of the realism, completely aware of the moment. And we talked for the longest time, or what seemed like the longest time ...

[WE ARE OUT ON THE HIGHWAY, CAREERING ALONG HIGHWAY 7 BETWEEN PETERBOROUGH AND OTTAWA. EPIC OUTCROPPINGS OF THE CANADIAN SHIELD SHOULDER THEIR WAY FROM THE EARTH, MASSIVE HILLSIDES OF ROCK PUNCTUATED BY THE SCRUBBY BRUSH AND STRAGGLING CONIFERS THAT CHARACTERIZE THIS SEMI-NORTHERN COUNTRYSIDE. AS THE LANDSCAPE STREAMS BY, THE CAMERA PANS AROUND AND WE SEE THAT WE ARE DRIVING IN THE ARTSPACE TRUCK. DAVID BIERK IS AT THE WHEEL AND ADDRESSES US DIRECTLY (AND THUS THE CAMERA) AS WE DRIVE.]

DAVID BIERK (AT THE WHEEL):

About 1975 my work shifted to a more specialized concern for certain formal aspects of painting – light, texture, colour – which resulted in the Canadian rock series, a series that came about from driving this highway through the heart of the Canadian Shield. Although there was a certain detachment from this kind of painting for me, a new objectivity, it could also be argued that the rock paintings – even though based to some extent on the photographs I took – were intensely personal and interpretive, very subjective – despite their roots in all this eon-long otherness ... Indeed, I suppose it's true that the larger and more generalized the subject, the smaller and more intensely revealing is one's attack upon it. [DIZZYING CLOSE-UP OF ROCKY LANDSCAPE SLIPPING BY, WHICH FADES TO A STUDIED EXAMINATION BY THE CAMERA OF THE PAINTING *ONE YEAR LATER* (1981). AS THE CAMERA ROLLS LIKE AN EYEBALL OVER THE CANVAS, WE HEAR THE NARRATOR – V/O.]

NARRATOR (V/O):

It is not a long distance from Bierk's up-close study of Canadian Shield rock formations, riven with crevices and fissures and veins, to his 'fold' paintings of the next few months – in the early

■ Dennis Tourbin

■ *Canadian Rock Series: Hwy. 7 near Innisville*, oil on canvas, 8' x 12', 1978. Collection: Fulcrum North, Peterborough, Ont.

■ *Canadian Rock Series: Georgian Bay*, oil on canvas, 8' x 12', 1980

■ *Canadian Rock Series, Hwy. 7 near Marmora*, oil on board 23½" x 34¼", 1976

1980s – in which Bierk physically folded the canvas and refolded it again and again, spray-painting the resulting dislocations so that the newly unfolded canvas now held the optically-convincing 'relief' segments that so much resembled, in their own way, the physicality of the rock outcroppings he had been painting. His painting *One Year Later*, from 1981, a summary work in many ways, employs the generalized foldscape (which is close in value to the real/texture of landscape) as a screen or support upon which are imposed portraits of John Lennon (murdered one year earlier) as well as a gridded disposition of other faces, presumably culture 'heroes' of Bierk's who are deemed fit to hold down the rest of the canvas (Emile Zola, Paul Gauguin, Vincent Van Gogh, Claude Monet, Gustave Courbet, Ingres, Sir Lawrence Alma-Tadema, and John Heartfield). *One Year Later* thus brings together the pastoral generalizations and infinite extendibility of the rock paintings, the pop-icon sensibility of *In Search of the American Dream*, the idea of *grid-organization* (which, in the mature paintings to come, will modulate into an epic employment of the diptych and triptych format). As Illi-Maria Tamplin, Director of the Art Gallery of Peterborough, has pointed out, the gridding also evokes the time-honoured image-transfer method which Bierk continues to make use of in his paintings of the last decade.

OFF-SCREEN INTERVIEWER:
You were painting all through the *Artspace* years?

DAVID BIERK:
Yes, but not enough. It was in November of 1986, after the Market Hall Building Project and six months of programming were securely in place, that I gave myself six months off to devote the time in a highly concentrated way to the production of new paintings and to approach commercial galleries in Canada and the USA and see if my work could find a place for itself out there beyond Artspace.

[CUT TO GARY MICHAEL DAULT ON CAMERA, BEING INTERVIEWED BY THE NOW-FAMILIAR OFF-SCREEN INTERVIEWER.]

GARY MICHAEL DAULT:
It is his *tenacity* I love. He just *never* gives up! (I have this horrible feeling it's un-Canadian, this relentlessness of David's.) I remember his telling me about his *epic journey* – it's almost mythical in its intensity – to New York, Los Angeles, and San Francisco in search of the outside world, in search of dealers, too, of course, but I really think it was a *fact-finding mission* ... asking to show his slides, getting turned down without a look nine times out of ten. Not giving up. Look at the Jan Turner Gallery story. It's his first stop in Los Angeles and he's attracted initially to the gallery because of its ad in *Artforum* (romantic landscapes by Bruce Everett), for gawdsake, and so he

- *One Year Later...*, acrylic and oil on canvas, 9' x 9', 1981. Collection: Art Gallery of Peterborough, Peterborough, Ont.

- *Convex Painting: To Earth #2*, acrylic on canvas, 5' x 5', 1981. Collection: Art Gallery of Algoma, Sault Ste. Marie, Ont.

- *Nineteen Eighty-One* (alternate installation II, with painted wall, Kingston Artists' Association), acrylic on canvas, 1982

waltzes into the gallery, asks to see Jan Turner (he doesn't even know if there *is* a Jan Turner; maybe she's some west coast version of O.K. Harris, right?), gives his spiel and his binder to the woman at the reception, is told Jan Turner (who *does* exist after all) is *really busy* and is going to New York the next day and couldn't possibly take the time but if he'd like to leave the portfolio perhaps? No, he wouldn't. He leaves the gallery, visits every other gallery in the city that day, finds himself winding wearily back to the Jan Turner at the end of the afternoon to take (how many of us would do this?) another shot. He pleads with the receptionist to take his portfolio overnight and show it to Ms. Turner. The woman agrees (reluctantly) but tells him not to hold his breath. Next morning, bright and early, in waltzes David, only to be given the thumbs down. Finally giving in to what looks like the inevitable, David thanks the receptionist and is about to try someplace else when she says she'll give it one more try and disappears from the front desk, heading back into Jan Turner territory with his binder of slides. He paces around for fifteen minutes. Then out from the sanctorum comes this chic and attractive woman who not only doesn't let him down easy but in fact tells him his work is wonderful and invites him – then and there – to join her stable of artists and furthermore to send some work down within the next two weeks so she can show it at the Los Angeles International Art Fair. David is in something like shock. He gets out of the gallery as quickly as he decently can before Jan Turner changes her mind. Outside, down the street, a safe distance away, he lets out a boyish whoop of joy, leaps into the air and clicks his heels together like Gene Kelly in *Singin' in the Rain* – all of which Jan Turner, much to David's mortification later, observes *after* all (and is greatly amused by). And so he's in.

OFF-SCREEN INTERVIEWER:
Against all odds, as they say.

GARY MICHAEL DAULT:
Except, of course, that the work is terrific.

■ Installation view, Jan Turner Gallery, 1990

■ *Art in America, Dec. 1987, Art in America, March 1988*, oil on canvas, 56" x 96", 1988
  Collection: McCarthy Tetrault, Toronto, Ont.

114

OFF-SCREEN INTERVIEWER:
And so he never returned to *Artspace*?

GARY MICHAEL DAULT:
He never did. And he says he's never regretted the decision. I think it was an amicable separation.

[SUPER-IMPOSITION IN HEAVY TYPE MAKES SLOW PROGRESS ACROSS THE SCREEN:]

WHAT IS BEING PAINTED?

[CUT TO DAVID BIERK'S STUDIO. GARY MICHAEL DAULT IS ENGAGED IN CONVERSATION WITH BIERK.]

GARY MICHAEL DAULT [EARNESTLY]:
There is a kind of curatorial persistence in you, a sense of completeness that appears to stop just before it billows out into obsessiveness.

DAVID BIERK [AMUSED]:
I hope so.

GARY MICHAEL DAULT [PERSEVERING]:
In a work like that series of inspired, slightly lunatic *Albert P. Ryder* paintings from 1990 – all those Ryders and *glosses* of Ryders – Ryders on the Storm – the pictures open out laterally like a scroll. Indeed, when you get to view all those Ryders together, it begins to read like some eerie alphabet ... it turns *sonic*, all those flashing 'phonetic' illuminations of yellow-green sky and gravy-coloured boats rocking across that continuum of sea ... and you get the feeling that at this point you are 'doing' Ryder, speaking to ...

DAVID BIERK:
Or with.

■ *The Toilers of the Sea, to Earth, Ryder and Fantin-Latour,*
  oil on canvas, photograph, 8'2" x 17'4" installed, 1990
■ *Ryder Boat Series*, Bess Cutler Gallery, New York, 1990

GARY MICHAEL DAULT:

Ryder, yes, and exhausting yourself upon Ryder, emptying Ryder out. Is this *homage* or a sort of *bringing-to-ground?*

DAVID BIERK:

I think there is, inevitably, in the idea of homage, the hidden or nested idea of traversing the maestro's trail and thus — as if brushwork were tracks in the snow — *inhabiting* what has gone before. This is quite a different thing, it seems to me, from the usual modalities of appropriation.

[CUT TO THE GREAT PAINTED STONE FACE OF ALEXANDER IN *ALEXANDER CONTEMPLATING WHY U.F.O.s DON'T LAND HERE ANYMORE: TO CASPAR DAVID FRIEDRICH, ALBERT BIERSTADT, JOHN WILLIAM CASILEAR, FREDERIC EDWIN CHURCH AND T.E. PFLIGER* (1987): WE EXPLORE THE SURFACE OF THE FACE, WE HEAR VOICES OVER ... A SORT OF STATELY ART-CRITICAL MINUET FOR SOUNDS.]

VOICE ONE:
Is this Alexander?

VOICE TWO:
Alexander who? Alexander the Great? We don't know what he looked like.

VOICE ONE:
It is not stone though it looks like stone. It is *painted* stone.

VOICE TWO:
No it's not. It's painted *paint.*

VOICE ONE:
Why are his eyes as blank as Little Orphan Annie's?

VOICE TWO:
That's the way the sculpture was.

■ *Alexander Contemplating Why U.F.O.s Don't Land Here Anymore: ... ,*
oil on canvas, 108" x 108", 1987. Collection: Marshall and Patricia Geller,
Los Angeles, Calif.

VOICE ONE:
Which sculpture? There is no sculpture.

VOICE TWO:
The photograph, then; that's the way the photograph was.

VOICE ONE:
What photograph?

VOICE TWO:
I suppose we're on our own here.

VOICE ONE:
What about those eyes? Aren't they inescapably the stuff of metaphor?

VOICE TWO:
I don't know about inescapably.

VOICE ONE:
What about the face's pitted stone texture?

VOICE TWO:
It's pitted paint, an antiqued patina of pure accomplishment by the painter ...

VOICE ONE:
Why show it off, though?

VOICE TWO:
Why not? But anyhow that's scarcely the point. The Alexander – that's who we are told it is – is answered by that filmstrip or soundtrack of landscapes ...

VOICE ONE:
How do you mean – answered?

VOICE TWO:
They're juxtaposed – one to the other and all of them to Alexander.

VOICE ONE:
So?

VOICE TWO:
So you have to deal with them, reconcile them, *make something* of them.

VOICE ONE:
Why?

VOICE TWO:
Because the artist chose to bring them together. Unless he was just sleepwalking, he has to have done so *for a reason*.

VOICE ONE:
But all the potential reasons seem *oppressive* to me, too tumbril-like. I can't go through all that stuff about how perhaps the non-seeing eyes of the conqueror have – what? – left the world in ruins (see the ruins in the landscapes) or have failed to quell the upthrusting loveliness of a later world, or that the lushness of the planetary world will always be threatened by a negating will like Alexander's ...

VOICE TWO:
Was Alexander's will negating? Aren't there better tyrants to hand than Alexander, if you want tyrants?

VOICE ONE:
Suppose we just *gave up* before the picture?

VOICE TWO:
Withhold interpretation? What results?

117

VOICE ONE:
A certain *dandification*. An aloofness that lets the painting swell like music and wash like poetry.

VOICE TWO:
What if we end up missing the point that way?

VOICE ONE:
What if we end up getting it that way? I don't think we ought to keep our eyes too close to the ground.

VOICE TWO:
I have no idea what that means.

VOICE ONE:
I don't believe you.

[CUT TO DAVID BIERK'S STUDIO: DAULT AND BIERK STILL IN CONVERSATION ... Dault is saying to Bierk that there is, after all, a difficulty in too much one-on-one reading of these later paintings. For example, in *Save the Planet/Autumn Sunset, to Keith and Caravaggio* (1989), where an ember-like sunset is held up for comparison or comment to a blown-up detail from a Caravaggio, an image of sleep, death, or defeat of some sort. There is here the possibility of a sort of stasis, or more acutely, a self-cancellation of the two sides of the painting as one merely becomes a modality of the other, this equalling that. And Bierk is replying that in the first place he *is* interested in the primary imagery the paintings afford. He is interested, for example, in the pressures of spiritual decline and the idea of the autumnal as some sort of penultimate state. So, the *accumulations* in a painting such as this one are knowable in themselves and need not be resisted as a way of preparing for the painting's potentially bigger metaphysical payload ... and Dault is suggesting that a painting like *New York Times Magazine February 10, 1985 to Jean Michel Basquiat and Manet* (1989) is easy – too easy – to read as a sorry anti-hymn to the enduring wonder of a Manet still-life inspected in the

■ *Save the Planet/Autumn Sunset, to Keith and Caravaggio,*
  oil on canvas, 60" x 123", 1989

■ *New York Times Magazine February 10, 1985 to Jean Michel Basquiat and Manet,*
  oil on canvas, 44½" x 61", 1989. Private collection

light of our thoughts about the transient fame (and commodified reputation) of Basquiat. But the painting seems more useful as a painterly performance of virtuoso surfaces. The 'depiction' of the reproduced colour-photo of Basquiat himself is as fine and as painterly as the vase of Manet flowers. So doesn't the painting speak more to a state wherein the painterly beat goes on than some carping lesson in the politics of greed or the fickleness inherent in the academic non-idea of *quality?* Bierk confirms that the pictures are much more useful as flaggings of the conceptual force of comparison itself as opposed to their status as some theatre of virtuosity … and so the talk goes …]

[THE CAMERA PANS LOVINGLY OVER THE SURFACES OF A NUMBER OF BIERK'S PAINTINGS, THAT PASTORAL EASE, THAT PICTORIAL GRAZING BEING INTERFERED WITH BY A CRAWL OF SUPERIMPOSED TEXT WHICH READS, IN PART:]

1. How hieratic is contemporary painting permitted to be? How heraldic? How altar-like?

2. Are the two sides of a diptych engaged inevitably in dialogue, or can they remain mute though inescapably juxtaposed? And if the latter, can there be an ethics of imagery that does not evade responsibility while nevertheless refusing the enactment of the confessional mode?

3. Where is the artist? Out back of the painting, whittling and paring his fingernails?

4. Is there anything to *expiate* in these pictures? There isn't any wish here to rid oneself of some curse of competence (surely not)? If not, then why do the paintings sometimes seem *mordant*, if not downright abashed by their art-historical grandeur?

[CUT TO GARY MICHAEL DAULT LOOKING AT A SMALL MANET BY DAVID BIERK. HE HOLDS IT IN HIS HANDS, STUDYING IT.]

- A Eulogy to Art (and Aspiration), Flash Art summer 1990, Kostabi, and Mondrian, oil on photographs and canvas, steel, 33" x 49", 1992. Private collection
- Art News, Oct. 1978 to Joseph Beuys and Manet, oil on canvas, 44½" x 61", 1989 Collection: Davies, Ward and Beck, Toronto, Ont.

GARY MICHAEL DAULT:

It's as desirable as any little Manet, a Manet drained of its monetary value and freed into the sybaritic joy of its own execution. [SUDDENLY HOLDING IT UP TO THE CAMERA] *Doesn't everybody want one of these?* Can't you *feel* it as pure desire? It makes desire itself a studiable force, and separates from the whole collector-curator act the hedonism of the object on its own. So what is this – a little paradigm of need? A single molecule of acquisitiveness?

[CUT TO DAVID BIERK, HANDLING A SIMILAR LITTLE MANET-MANQUÉ OF HIS OWN DEVISING …]

DAVID BIERK:

Of course the paint-handling is mine, not Manet's. I might take his composition, his imagery, his light and transparency and so on, but the trace of the painter's hand leads back to me, and the drag of the painter's brush through the pigment is a drag I feel in my own arm.

GARY MICHAEL DAULT:

It's as though you have covered a very palpable dream of a Manet with a scrim of your own motion as a painter.

[CLOSE-UP OF THE PAINTING *A EULOGY TO ART, DAVID WATCHING, TO FANTIN-LATOUR* (1990).]

OFF-SCREEN INTERVIEWER:

Some of the best of them are about art itself, are they not? About how art gets made, what befalls art, what remains, where it resides.

OFF-SCREEN QUESTION:

What is meant by Bierk's multi-valent rubric "In the Absence of Paradise"?

[SCENE: DAVID BIERK'S STUDIO. WE SEE A CLOSE-UP OF A LOADED BRUSH RASPING PIGMENT INTO THE BURGEONING IMAGE OF A RECREATED PASSAGE FROM A MANTEGNA. WE

■ *Fleurs dans un vase*, from the *Last Flowers of Manet* series, oil on canvas, 22" x 14½", 1987. Collection: James Lodge and Associates, Irvine, Calif.

■ *A Eulogy/Art and Life, to Eakins and Manet*, oil on canvas, oil on linen, steel, 20" x 39", 1993

CONTINUE TO WATCH THE BRUSH SMOOTHING, LICKING, CARESSING THE PIGMENT INTO PLACE, AS WE HEAR GARY MICHAEL DAULT (OVER THE ACT OF PAINTING):]

GARY MICHAEL DAULT (V/O):

In the absence of Paradise, we have certain shards shored against our ruins, have we not? There is something of the paradisiacal *in the defeat of dialogue* (as, for example, in the later diptychs and triptychs), where nothing mutually illuminates nothing but where everything is set adrift *in a continual present*. In painting, the past can be reclaimed over and over again until it fills up (like a vessel) into total and *utter availability*. [WE SEE BIERK'S FACE. WE SEE HIM INSPECTING WHAT HE HAS DONE. WE SEE HIM TURN TO THE CAMERA. HE ADDRESSES THE CAMERA DIRECTLY.]

DAVID BIERK [SMILING]:

Or perhaps that's all a dream, an essay, the past and the present – maybe even the future – of art, all reclaimable by the force of admiration and respect … A kind of reverie … [FADE TO BLACK]

[FOLLOWED BY CERTAIN NOURISHING CREDITS]

– FIN –

EPILOGUE:

There I am in Los Angeles at the behest of Warner Brothers, whose expectation it is (not unreasonably I suppose) that if they subject me to enough room service and set me adrift on a wide Sargasso Sea of complimentary booze, I will come back to Toronto and say not unkind things about the film they are momentarily releasing – in this case John Badham's remake of 'La Femme Nikita', a star turn for Bridget Fonda called 'Point of No Return'. Los Angeles seems a point of no return all by itself, if you ask me. I am swooning back on the king-size bed in my hotel room, watching movies on video one after another so that they are sort of running together in what is left of my mind, when the only friend I have in L.A. – a composer named Sharon Smith – swoops down upon me and (in the nick of time) spirits me out of the hotel and out into what she assures me is the Real Los Angeles. Sharon is a composer and a music editor for the movies, and for her the real Hollywood is the hands-on nuts-and-bolts Hollywood where real people make real things happen. We visit the M.O.C.A., take an art walk through downtown L.A. (Rauschenberg, Stella, Bruce Nauman). We end up outside the Sheraton Grande Hotel – which houses a huge David Bierk painting.

ADDITIONAL FOOTAGE:

[THIS OUGHT TO BE FILMED, AND SINCE THIS FILM IS ENTIRELY FICTITIOUS THERE IS NOTH-
ING EASIER TO DO.] There are three of us: Sharon Smith, her friend, a local L.A. painter named
Albert Beach, and me. We are just outside the hotel. The huge doors open to admit us and we
file in. [THE CAMERA IS BEHIND US, FOLLOWING US INTO THE GIGANTIC LOBBY, SEARCHING
– AS WE ARE – FOR DAVID'S PICTURE.]

GARY MICHAEL DAULT [LOOKING WILDLY AROUND]:
Where is it? It's supposed to be big. David said it was a really big painting.

SHARON SMITH [PRESSING UP BEHIND DAULT]:
I don't see anything that looks like a painting.

ALBERT BEACH [BEHIND SHARON SMITH]:
Me neither.

[THEN, SUDDENLY, IT IS THERE BEFORE THEM. THIS PAINTING IS SO VAST THEY COULDN'T
SEE IT; THEY WERE LOOKING FOR SOMETHING WHICH MIGHT CONCEIVABLY BE HUNG
WITHIN THE SORT OF SPACE THE PAINTING TAKES UP. THE PAINTING IS TOO MACRO TO BE
IMMEDIATELY IDENTIFIED AS A PAINTING. BY NOW ALL THREE OF THE PILGRIMS HAVE MADE
CERTAIN SPATIAL ADJUSTMENTS, CERTAIN ALLOWANCES OF SCALE. SO HAS THE CAMERA.
THE CAMERA PULLS UP TO THE BASE OF THE PAINTING AND BEGINS A SLOW ADMIRING
PAN OVER ITS EPIC SURFACE.]

ALBERT BEACH [AWED]:
My gawd.

SHARON SMITH:
It's big, all right!

DAULT [DELIGHTED AND BASKING IN THE REFLECTED GLOW OF DAVID'S SUCCESS]:
It's great. See how [EVER THE TEACHER] the Vermeer head floats so assuredly over the landscape – that lush, Luminist landscape that David seems so drawn to! See how strange it is, but
how authoritative? You know [TURNING TO SHARON SMITH], it's really odd how un-surrealistic
the thing is, don't you think? I mean, wouldn't you think of this as a piece of surrealism if somebody just described it to you?

SHARON SMITH [DETERMINED NOW – HAVING RIGHTED HERSELF SOMEWHAT – TO CRACK THIS THING]:

What landscape is this?

GARY MICHAEL DAULT [NOT SURE AND NOT CARING A LOT JUST NOW]:

Cole, Church, one of those guys David likes … but at this gigantic scale!!

ALBERT BEACH [MOVING UP CLOSER TO THE PAINTING'S SURFACE]:

There isn't any stinting … I mean this is a really generous, hotly worked-up surface …

SHARON SMITH [ADMIRINGLY]:

Incredibly detailed.

GARY MICHAEL DAULT [ALSO ADMIRINGLY]:

And surmounted by that wonderful serene floating Vermeer …

[ALL THREE OF THEM STEP BACK AGAIN, ALMOST AS IF IT WERE NECESSARY TO DISCUSS THE PAINTING IN CAMERA, AWAY FROM ITS FORCEFULNESS. THEY TALK ABOUT THE PAINTING AS SHEER METHODOLOGY, ABOUT HOW IT IS MADE UP OF NINE EQUAL SECTIONS BROUGHT TOGETHER TO GIVE IT ITS FINAL FORMAT. THEY TALK ABOUT HOW FULLY-DECLARED THE PAINTING IS, HOW WHAT THERE IS TO GAZE UPON IS WHAT THERE IS, HOW LITTLE FUDGING THERE IS (THOUGH NONE OF THEM CAN FATHOM WHAT THAT MIGHT CONSIST OF EVEN IF IT WERE POSSIBLE), HOW OPEN AND (IF IT CAN BE PUT THIS WAY) GUILELESS THE PAINTING IS. IT IS AGREED BY ALL THREE THAT IT IS THE PAINTING'S FUNDAMENTAL INNOCENCE THAT PRECLUDES ITS HAVING A SURREALIST PROGRAM.]

SHARON SMITH [HER EYES STILL FIXED UPON THE PAINTING]:

So, listen, is this de-constructivism?

GARY MICHAEL DAULT [TAKEN BY SURPRISE]:

Not at all.

ALBERT BEACH [RESOLUTE]:

Not at all.

GARY MICHAEL DAULT [STARTING TO GET SELF-CONSCIOUS WITH THE POSSIBILITIES]:

Maybe – sort of. I mean, only in the sense that the painting's fully-laid-bare formatting hides nothing about the way it was made. But the oddness of it, its imagistic cheek, doesn't seem to help with any kind of dismantling of its meaning. There's a strange kind of easeful pride coalesced within that buoyant Vermeer that speaks of a certain kind of virtuoso expansiveness, a certain kind of aesthetic heroism that …

[THE CAMERA BLEEDS THROUGH TO A CLOSE-UP OF THIS TYPEWRITER AND THIS TEXT – BEING TYPED. WHATEVER WE SEE ON THE SCREEN NOW IS SIMPLY THIS ACT OF TYPING, THIS LINE OF THOUGHT ACCUMULATING ON THE PAGE.]

… entirely precludes the aggressive modesty of any deconstructivist act. In a sense, David Bierk's modernity – or post-modernity – is achieved as a by-product of his approaching asymptotically closer and closer to the very life of the pictures (and the artists) from the past that enthrall him. His unfurling act of homage is, more and more, some lever by which the art of the past and his own art can be made congruent. What keeps him contemporary? His inability and his unwillingness to escape from the present. His decision to tough it out in the present by, for example, permitting and employing grace-notes of modernist practice within his paintings (steel frames around delicately-realized still-lifes from history, in some instances). His relentless pairings and comparings and radical juxtapositions (though this last is in itself a plundering – for different purposes – of a surrealist tic).

[THE PHONE RINGS. IT IS DAVID BIERK. HE IS EXCITED AT JUST HAVING FINISHED A PAINTING WHICH HE HAS EXECUTED ENTIRELY ON STEEL PLATE. HE IS ECSTATIC ABOUT THE SENSITIVE RESPONSE OF THE BRUSH WHICH IS PLAYED BACK BY THE UNYIELDINGNESS OF THE UNINFLECTED, IMPASSIVE STEEL SURFACE. HE GIVES ME THE IMPRESSION THAT THERE IS SUDDENLY SOME NEW, ACCELERATED DELICACY AVAILABLE TO HIM – GENERATED (PARADOXICALLY) BY THE BRUT FIELD OF THE METAL. 'YOU WAIT!' HE TELLS ME GLEEFULLY, "YOU WAIT!"]

A FANTASY ABOUT DAVID BIERK

It's midnight. I'm tired now and I want to go to sleep, but there's an intrusive fantasy that precludes it, a sort of elaborate conceit about David and his painting which will not go away. What happens is that David has moved so close to the spirit of what he loves from his embattled eyrie in the late twentieth century – his contemporaneity now inextricably bound up with the act of choosing and inhabiting some epic resting place from another art-century – that he ends up, like the brilliant 'Pierre Menard' who, in Borges' story, writes a segment of Cervantes' *Don Quixote* without duplicating the original (an act of un-creation), painting – with an utterly believable spontaneity and subtlety – 'Courbet's The Painter's Studio, a Real Allegory Summing Up Seven Years of my Life as an Artist.' David's Courbet is exactly like Courbet's Courbet in every detail, even in the typographies of its brushwork. The original Courbet is now – like the original Don Quixote – 'slightly archaic'. David's Courbet is brilliantly, exhaustingly, horrifyingly new. –GARY MICHAEL DAULT

125

DAVID BIERK

Born

Appleton, Minnesota, 1944
Immigrated to Canada, 1972
Canadian Citizen, 1978

Resides

Peterborough, Ontario

Studied

California College of Arts & Crafts,
Oakland, Calif.
B.A., Humboldt State University, Arcata, Calif.
M.F.A., Humboldt State University, Arcata, Calif.
Teaching Certificate, University of Toronto,
Toronto, Ont.

Related Experience

Founder & Director of Artspace,
Peterborough, Ont., 1974-87

SELECTED SOLO EXHIBITIONS

1994   Wynick/Tuck Gallery, Toronto, Ont.
Diane Farris Gallery, Vancouver, B.C.
Erickson and Elins Fine Art, San Francisco, Calif.
Rodman Hall Arts Centre, St. Catharines, Ont.
Niagara Artists' Centre, St. Catharines, Ont.
Leedy-Voulkos Gallery, Kansas City, Mo.

1993   Adams-Middleton Gallery, Dallas, Tex.
Galerie L'autre équivoque, Ottawa, Ont.
The Lowe Gallery, Atlanta, Ga.
Dayton Art Institute, Dayton, Ohio
University of Waterloo Art Gallery, Waterloo, Ont.
Russell Gallery, Lindsay, Ont.
Glendon Gallery, York University, Toronto, Ont.

1993   Wynick/Tuck Gallery, Toronto, Ont.
Thomson Gallery, Minneapolis, Minn.
Diane Farris Gallery, Vancouver, B.C.

1992   Barclay Simpson Fine Arts Gallery, Lafayette, Calif.
Diane Farris Gallery, Vancouver, B.C.
Struve Gallery, Chicago, Ill.
Wynick/Tuck Gallery, Toronto, Ont.
Ottawa Art Gallery, Ottawa, Ont.

1991   Arts Sutton, Sutton, P.Q.
Wynick/Tuck Gallery (small gallery), Toronto, Ont.
Art Gallery of Algoma, Sault Ste. Marie, Ont.
Art Gallery of Peterborough, Peterborough, Ont.
Robert Thomson Gallery, Minneapolis, Minn.
Felicita Foundation, San Diego, Calif.

1990   Wynick/Tuck Gallery, Toronto, Ont.
Susan Whitney Gallery, Regina, Sask.
Bess Cutler Gallery, New York, N.Y.
Jan Turner Gallery, Los Angeles, Calif.

1989   Thomson Gallery, Minneapolis, Minn.
Wynick/Tuck Gallery, Toronto, Ont.
Diane Farris Gallery, Vancouver, B.C.
'Painted Photomontages', Wynick/Tuck Gallery,
Toronto, Ont.
Iannetti-Lanzone Gallery, San Francisco, Calif.

1988   Gallery 101, Ottawa, Ont.
Wynick/Tuck Gallery, Toronto, Ont.
Odette Gilbert Gallery, London, England

1987   Jan Turner Gallery, Los Angeles, Calif.

1981-83   'David Bierk: Ten Years', Peterborough and touring: Sudbury, Sault Ste. Marie, Windsor, Lindsay, Ottawa, Stratford.

1975,76   Nancy Poole's Studio, Toronto, Ont.

1975   St. Lawrence College Art Gallery, Kingston, Ont.
MacKenzie Gallery, Trent University,
Peterborough, Ont.

SELECTED GROUP EXHIBITIONS

1994   Seattle Art Fair, Seattle, Wash.

1993   'Approaching the 21st Century', Joseph D. Carrier
Gallery, North York, Ont.

Canadian Exhibit at Expo, Seoul, South Korea

'An American Renaissance', The Lowe Gallery,
Atlanta, Ga.

'A Gallery Retrospective', California Center for the
Arts, Escondido, Calif.

'The Purloined Image', Flint Institute of the Arts,
Flint, Mich.

'Landscapes I/Paysages I', Galerie L'autre
équivoque, Ottawa, Ont.

'Highlights', Brown-Forman Corporation,
Louisville, Kentucky

'Where is Here?', Art Gallery of Peterborough, Ont.

'New Landscape', The Gallery Three Zero,
New York, N.Y.

'Quotations', Aldrich Museum, Ridgefield, Conn.;
Art Institute, Dayton, Ohio.

Seattle Art Fair, Seattle, Wash.

1992   Security Pacific Gallery, San Francisco, Calif.

Chicago International Art Fair, Chicago, Ill.

1991   'Contemporary Landscape', MetLife Gallery,
New York, N.Y.

Chicago International Art Fair, Chicago, Ill.

'The Big Picture', Diane Farris Gallery,
Vancouver, B.C.

1990   'Horizons', Pfizer Inc., New York, N.Y.
(MOMA Extension Exhibition)

'Contemporary Landscape', ABC Television Inc.,
New York, N.Y. (MOMA Extension Exhibition)

'Critical Revisions', Bess Cutler Gallery,
New York, N.Y.

1990   Chicago International Art Fair, Chicago, Ill.

1989   'Contemporary Landscape: New Perspectives',
Hearst Gallery, St. Mary's College, Moraga, Calif.

'Photomontage/Photocollage: The Changing
Picture 1920-1989', Jan Turner Gallery,
Los Angeles, Calif.

1988   'Landscape Anthology', Grace Borgenicht Gallery,
New York, N.Y.

1988   'Life Stories: Myth, Fiction & History in
Contemporary Art', Henry Art Gallery,
Seattle, Wash.

1987   'David Bierk, Malcolm Rains & Jeffrey Spalding',
Diane Farris Gallery, Vancouver, B.C.

1987   'The Current Landscape', Felicita Foundation,
San Diego, Calif.

1987   'Painting', Jan Turner Gallery, Los Angeles, Calif.

1987   'David Bierk & Jeffrey Spalding', North Bay
Arts Centre, North Bay, Ont.

1987   'Nature Redefined: A Cultural Perspective', Piezo
Electric Gallery, New York, N.Y.; Segal Steinberg
Gallery, Montreal, P.Q.

1986-92   Los Angeles International Art Fair, Los Angeles, Calif.

1986   'Artspace/Memorial University Art Gallery
Exchange', Peterborough,Ont.; St. John's, Nfld.

1986   'The Romantic Landscape Now', Artspace,
Peterborough, Ont.; Art Gallery of Algoma, Sault
Ste. Marie, Ont.; Southern Alberta Art Gallery,
Lethbridge, Alta.; Kamloops Art Gallery,
Kamloops, B.C.; Nova Corporation, Calgary, Alta.;
Surrey Art Gallery, Surrey, B.C.

1985   'Atmospheric Synthesis', Art Gallery of
Peterborough, Peterborough, Ont.

1985   Inaugural Exhibition, Artspace, Peterborough, Ont.

1984   'Edge & Image', Concordia University Art Gallery,
Montreal, P.Q.

1983	'New Perspectives: Landscapes', Art Gallery at Harbourfront, Toronto, Ont.	London Regional Art Gallery, London, Ont.
1982	'Arts Against Repression', Artspace, Peterborough, Ont.; Brock University, St. Catharines, Ont.	Art Gallery of Peterborough, Peterborough, Ont.

1983   'New Perspectives: Landscapes', Art Gallery at
        Harbourfront, Toronto, Ont.

1982   'Arts Against Repression', Artspace,
        Peterborough, Ont.; Brock University,
        St. Catharines, Ont.

1979   'The Texture of Our Land', Art Gallery of
        Peterborough, Peterborough, Ont.

1978/80 'Reflecting A Rural Consciousness',
        The Art Gallery at Harbourfront, Toronto, Ont.;
        Artspace, Peterborough, Ont.; Kingston Artists'
        Centre, Kingston, Ont.; SAW Gallery, Ottawa,
        Ont.; Art Gallery of Windsor, Windsor, Ont.;
        Hall Walls, Buffalo, N.Y.; Canadian Cultural
        Centre, Paris, France

1977   'Ontario Now No. 2', Art Gallery of Hamilton,
        Hamilton, Ont.

1976   'Artspace Steps Out', Ontario touring

1976   'Forum '76', Montreal Museum of Fine Arts,
        Montreal, P.Q.

1975   'Monument to Miniature', Artspace, Peterborough,
        Ont.

1974   '1er Acte/New Talent', Marlborough Godard
        Gallery, Montreal, P.Q.

1974   'Aspects of Realism', Gallery Moos, Toronto, Ont.;
        Montreal, P.Q.

SELECTED PRINCIPAL COLLECTIONS

National Gallery of Canada, Ottawa, Ont.
Art Gallery of Ontario, Toronto, Ont.
Canadian Museum of Contemporary Photography, Ottawa, Ont.
Art Gallery of Windsor, Windsor, Ont.
Edmonton Art Gallery, Edmonton, Alta.
Art Gallery of Hamilton, Hamilton, Ont.

London Regional Art Gallery, London, Ont.
Art Gallery of Peterborough, Peterborough, Ont.
Brampton Art Gallery, Brampton, Ont.
Canada Council Art Bank, Ottawa, Ont.
External Affairs and International Trade Canada, Ottawa, Ont.
Trent University, Peterborough, Ont.
Humboldt State University, Arcata, Calif.
Canadian Postal Museum, Ottawa, Ont.
City of Peterborough, Ont.
Bank of America, Toronto, Ont.
Olympia & York Developments Ltd., Toronto, Ont.
McCarthy Tetrault, Toronto, Ont.
U.S. Trust Corporation, New York, N.Y.
Canadian Imperial Bank of Commerce, Toronto, Ont.
Petro-Canada, Calgary, Alta.
Prudential-Bache, New York, N.Y.
Redpath Mining Associates, North Bay, Ont.
Touche, Ross & Co., Los Angeles, Calif.
Steinberg Ltd., Montreal, P.Q.
Jones Heward Investments Management, Montreal, P.Q.
Power Corporation, Montreal, P.Q.
Nova Corporation, Calgary, Alta.
Fulcrum North Inc., Peterborough, Ont.
Les Trois Marches, Versailles, France
Grand Hyatt Hotel, Hong Kong
Hyatt Regency Hotel, Chicago, Ill.
Intercontinental Hotels, Toronto, Ont.
Reader's Digest, Pleasantville, N.Y.
Metropolitan Life, New York, N.Y.
Central Guaranty Trust, Toronto, Ont.
Toronto Dominion Bank, Toronto, Ont.
McDermott, Will & Emery, Chicago, Ill.
N.Y.N.E.X., White Plains, N.Y.
W.R. Grace Inc., New York, N.Y.
Becton Dickinson Corporation, Franklin Lakes, N.J.

Progressive Corporation, Mayfield, Ohio.

Jon Bon Jovi, N.J.

Axl Rose, Los Angeles, Calif.

Edward R. Downe, Jr., New York, N.Y.

Health Net, Woodland Hills, Calif.

Dayton Art Institute, Dayton, Ohio.

Atlantic Richfield Corporation, Los Angeles, Calif.

Microsoft Corporation, Redmond, Wash

COMMISSIONS

Canada Post Corporation, Ottawa, Ont.

Sir Sandford Fleming College, Peterborough, Ont.

I.O.D.E., Peterborough, Ont.

Canadore College, North Bay, Ont.

Music Gallery, Toronto, Ont.

Ministry of Revenue, Oshawa, Ont.

Ministry of Health, Kingston, Ont.

Stitzel Company, San Francisco, Calif.

Princess Hotels Ltd., Scottsdale, Ariz.

Atlantic Records, New York, N.Y.

Ramada Renaissance Hotel, Los Angeles, Calif.

Sheraton Grande Hotel, Los Angeles, Calif.

Gardner, Carton & Douglas Inc., Chicago, Ill.

N.T.T., Tokyo, Japan

RJR Nabisco, New York, N.Y.

AWARDS

1974,86,87	Canada Council Project Grant
1975,83,85	Canada Council 'B' Grant
1976-89	Ontario Arts Council Materials Assistance Grant
1978	Canada Council Short Term Grant
1979	Canada Council Artist-in-Residence, North Bay, Ont.
1979,80	Ontario Association of Art Galleries (O.A.A.G.),
1979,80	Best Overall Gallery Image (1st Prize)
1979	O.A.A.G. Newsletter Design (1st Prize)
1980	O.A.A.G. Catalogue Design (1st Prize)
1980,81	O.A.A.G. Poster Design (1st Prize)
1981	Canada Council Artist-in-Residence, St. Catharines, Ont.
1991	Best Album Cover of the Year, RAW Magazine
1992	Hon. Mention, Album Cover of the Year, Rolling Stone Magazine Annual Music Awards

CONTRIBUTORS

ILLI-MARIA TAMPLIN is the Director of the Art Gallery of Peterborough and was the chief curator for the exhibition 'In the Absence of Paradise' at the Art Gallery of Peterborough in 1991. Her essay, 'David Bierk: Observer, Painter, Curator, Realist, Romantic, Dreamer, or How does photography, that secondary reality, feed the primary reality of painting?', won the Ontario Association of Art Galleries' award for curatorial writing in 1992.

DENNIS TOURBIN is a poet, painter and performance artist who is interested in the exploration of language as a visual medium. His visual poems and painted plays have been exhibited throughout Canada, in the U.S.A., France, Belgium and England. Tourbin's work is in the collections of The National Gallery of Canada, The Canada Council Art Bank, External Affairs and International Trade Canada and the National Archives of Canada.

DANIEL SHARP is a painter, writer, father and cultural bureaucrat living in Ottawa. His interest in Bierk's painting is rooted in their longtime friendship. Sharp is also motivated by the fascination he finds in the issues raised in Bierk's work: cultural dislocation and identity, the contemporary interpretation of art history, and the Canadian possibilities for the expression of an independent regional voice and vision.

GARY MICHAEL DAULT is a Toronto writer and art critic. His most recent book is 'Children in Photography – 150 Years'. He has recently completed a six-hour television documentary about the Vatican for Sir Peter Ustinov.

ADDITIONAL CREDITS

William Wilson, Peterborough – principal photography; James Franklin, Los Angeles – photography; Thomas Moore, Thomas Moore Photography Inc., Toronto; Douglas Webb, Peterborough – photography; Brian Proctor, Port Hope – photography; Rollyn Puterbaugh, Dayton, Ohio – photography; Ken Fraser, Peterborough – photography; Ray Bourgeois, Peterborough Examiner, Peterborough – photography; Mark Seliger, Straight Arrow Publishers, Inc. – photography; Aimee Rentmeester, Los Angeles – photography; David Vance, Miama – photography; Tim Wickens Photography, Ottawa – re-photography; Yvan Boulerice, The Canada Council Art Bank, Ottawa – photography; John Moffat, Ottawa – photography; Diana Tyndale, Piranha Communications, Ottawa – proofreading and editing; Ron Webb and Blake Royston, Studio Colour Group Inc., Ottawa; Krista Nicholds, Dollco Printing, Ottawa; Tim Wilson, Mangajin Books, Toronto; Vera Novacek, Art Gallery of Peterborough – bookkeeping; Dominic Hardy, Peterborough – translation; Edward Czmielewski, Peterborough – technical assistance.